I0817146

The Mystical Meaning of NUMBERS

IN SACRED SCRIPTURE

SAINT ISIDORE OF SEVILLE

Translated by Fr. Robert Nixon, OSB

TAN Books

Gastonia, North Carolina

Translated by Fr. Robert Nixon, OSB

Cover design by Jordan Avery

Cover image: *Adoration of the Trinity*, Albrecht Dürer (1471–1528), 1511, oil on lime panel. Kunsthistorisches Museum. Public Domain via Google Arts & Culture / Wikimedia Commons.

Interior Image: *Representation of Saint Isidore of Seville (560 or 570 - 636) with his brothers Saint Leandre and Saint Fulgence*. 19th century (engraving) Photo © The Holbarn Archive / Bridgeman Images.

ISBN: 978-1-5051-3662-3
Kindle ISBN: 978-1-5051-3736-1
ePUB ISBN: 978-1-5051-3735-4

Published in the United States by
TAN Books
PO Box 269
Gastonia, NC 28053

www.TANBooks.com

Printed in the United States of America

"In measure, and in number, and in weight Thou hast ordered all things."

—WISDOM 11:21

CONTENTS

TRANSLATOR'S INTRODUCTION

FOR THE CHRISTIAN, the depths of meaning contained within Sacred Scripture are immense and ever-expanding. And among the levels of meaning of Scripture are those which pertain not simply to the literal circumstances and historical events, but also those which are traditionally termed the allegorical or analogical. These latter two terms refer to the mystical or symbolic spiritual significations contained within the various details of the text.

Indeed, as the word inspired by the Holy Spirit, valuable and illuminating meanings may be gathered from virtually every one of the elements of Scripture. Of great importance among these potentially meaningful elements is *number*. Very often in the writings of both the Old and New Testaments, numbers are specified with great care and detail by the sacred authors, highlighting the fact that they were understood to have real significance in shedding light upon the deeper or mystical symbolism of the text.

From the times of classical antiquity and through the entire Middle Ages, it was understood that number was something inherently spiritual, with its meanings extending far beyond the mere identification or quantification of material objects or durations of time or space. For the Pythagoreans and Platonists of the classical world, as well as the ancient Hebrews, the universe was a harmonious and precisely numbered ordered system, reflecting through this numerical ordering the glory and beauty of the Deity. This sense of the deeper importance of number as a sign of divine ordering continued among Christian writers and thinkers, according perfectly with the conception of God as the ultimate source of all that exists, and whose every work is done with an eternal and transcendent Wisdom.

The author of the work presented in this present volume on the significance and meaning of number in Sacred Scripture is Saint Isidore of Seville (560–636), a Doctor of the Church and outstanding and encyclopedic scholar, who served as bishop of Seville. In his most famous work, the magisterial compendium on *Etymology,* Saint Isidore himself reflects upon this symbolic value of numbers in the following terms:[1]

1 *Libri Etymologiarum,* III:4.

> The importance of numbers should not be overlooked, and in many places in the Sacred Scriptures mystical meanings shine forth through them with radiance and illumination. It is to the glory of God and with deep significance that Scripture affirms: "In measure, and in number, and in weight Thou hast ordered all things."[2] And if number and quantity were to be taken away from creation, all things would lose their forms and cease to exist.

It should be noted that in his celebrated work on etymology (comprising some twenty books), Isidore deals not only with the origin and connection between words themselves, but presents what is virtually a complete and comprehensive encyclopedia of all forms and branches of knowledge in existence—an almost miraculous and superhuman feat at the time of its authorship. It is for this reason that Isidore was fittingly declared to be the patron saint of the internet by Pope Saint John Paul II in 1997.

As well as Saint Isidore's work on *The Mystical Meaning of Numbers in Sacred Scripture,* included also in this volume is a short biography life of the saint, taken from the Tridentine Breviary. The life story of the saint is itself inspiring, and he showed himself always to be an ardent devotee and defender of the truth (both as a scholar, teacher

2 Wis. 11:21.

and fighter of heresies), as well as a wise and effective bishop of the Church.

Fortunately, the original text of Saint Isidore's treatise is readily understood by a general reader, and only a basic knowledge of arithmetic is assumed, with the relationships and procedures he notes not going far beyond simple addition, subtraction, multiplication, and division. However, particular passages do ask of the reader close concentration and reflection, and his rich grounding in philosophical thinking is often apparent. Notes have been added where it seems as if an explanation might be useful, or when further information helps to clarify, contextualize, or illustrate the meaning. The source of the Latin text from which the translation has been made is the Migne *Patrologia Latina* LXXXIII:179–200.

It is the sincere hope of the translator that this fascinating and illuminating work will serve to deepen the contemplation of the riches of meaning of numbers within Sacred Scriptures for the reader, and lead him, with the help of the Holy Spirit, to an ever-deeper penetration of its hidden and holy treasures.

Fr. Robert Nixon, OSB
Abbey of the Most Holy Trinity,
New Norcia, Western Australia

THE LIFE OF ST. ISIDORE OF SEVILLE

From the *Breviarium Romanum ex Decreto SS. Concilii Tridentini Restitutum*

ISIDORE, A SPANIARD by nation, and a great Doctor of the Church, was born in Cartagena [in c. 560]. His father was a man called Severianus, who was the duke of the province. He was educated in piety and the liberal arts by Leander of Seville and Fulgentius of Cartagena, his brothers. He came to master the Greek, Latin, and Hebrew languages, and became an outstanding scholar, unrivalled in his knowledge of both sacred and secular literature. He manifested also all forms of Christian virtue in an exemplary and admirable manner.

Translator's note

Saint Leander and Saint Fulgentius were both brothers of Isidore. The former served as bishop of Seville (and was succeeded in this role after his death by Isidore), while the latter was bishop of Cartagena. Both of them, particularly Leander, have also left very significant writings.

While he was still a youth, Isidore set about combatting and refuting the heresy of Arianism, which was still widespread among the Gothic and Visigothic peoples who inhabited Spain. He posited himself openly as an opponent of the Arians and fought against their errors so tirelessly that many of the heretics plotted to kill him, but he willingly faced peril to his own life to defend the truth.

Translator's note

The Arians did not accept the co-eternal status of Christ as the Son of God, but believed rather that He was the first among created beings, sharing in the divine nature, but not equal to or consubstantial with God the Father. In late antiquity and the early Middle Ages, they were widespread and powerful in north Africa and Europe. By Isidore's time, they still survived in Spain, being supported by many leaders of the Goths and Visigoths who inhabited much of Spain.

When his older brother Leander, the bishop of Seville, passed away, Isidore accepted the episcopal throne of the great city. He did so reluctantly, in obedience both to the urging and encouragement of the king, Reccaredus, and the acclamation and support of the clergy and people of

Seville. The Pope, Saint Gregory the Great, not only confirmed and approved his selection, but also personally gifted him with a pallium, appointing Isidore as Vicar Apostolic for the whole of Spain.

In his role as bishop, Saint Isidore was faithful, humble, patient, merciful, and solicitous both for the discipline and well-being of the clergy and the devotion and piety of all the faithful. Indeed, no words could describe his diligence and indefatigable efforts in promoting and defending the faith, both by his writings and by the shining example of his own personal virtue.

Saint Isidore was an ardent promoter of monastic life throughout Spain. He brought about a tremendous growth in the contemplative life, constructing many new monasteries as well as colleges run by monasteries, where students could devote themselves in peace to the cultivation of the studies of both sacred and literary learning. A great many disciples flocked to him for instruction, which this erudite and holy man willingly provided. His students included Saint Ildephonsus, who became bishop of Toledo, and Saint Braulius, who became bishop of Zaragoza.

Saint Isidore convened a Council of the Church in Spain [the Second Council of Seville, of November, 619], in response to the heresy of the Acephali, which was then emerging as a threat to the faith in his land. Using eloquent and irrefutable arguments, he convincingly dismantled the erroneous positions of the Acephali.

Translator's note

The word 'Acephalus' literally means 'without a head.' The term has been applied to numerous heretical and schismatic groups throughout history, and indicates a refusal to accept the authority of the legitimate bishops or patriarchs, or the authentic Magisterium of the Church and its Councils. In this case, the Acephali in Spain at the time were influenced by a certain Syrian cleric who rejected the teachings of the Council of Chalcedon on the union of the divine and human natures of Christ.

Such was the reputation and esteem in which Isidore was held that, only sixteen years after his death, the whole Synod of the Spanish Church, assembled together at Toledo under the leadership of the wise and holy Saint Ildephonsus, agreed unanimously that it would be fitting for him to be declared a saint and a Doctor of the Church. For, indeed, he was universally considered to be the most learned man of his age and worthy of veneration both for his sanctity of life and wisdom of doctrine. Saint Braulius, bishop of Zaragoza, informed the Roman Pontiff, Gregory the Great, of this sentiment and desire. Saint Gregory not only enthusiastically agreed to this, but also dedicated the whole of Spain to the patronage of the apostle Saint James at that time.

Among his many writings, Isidore composed a notable and celebrated book of *Etymologies.* He also wrote countless other volumes on Sacred Scripture, Church doctrine, history, literature, and the natural sciences. These works were so expertly written, orthodox, and masterly in all regards that Pope Saint Leo IV declared that they should be given similar authority and respect as was given to the writings of Saint Augustine and Saint Jerome.

Leo IV recommended the writings of Saint Isidore in particular when it came to matters of the interpretation and application of Canon Law, and a great many of Isidore's opinions and judgements are now incorporated within the laws of the universal Church.

Saint Isidore convened also the Fourth Council of Toledo [633], which is the most celebrated Council in the history of Spain.

Translator's note

This Fourth Council of Toledo declared the mutual bond of respect and loyalty which bound the Spanish monarchy and the Catholic Church. It also decreed the establishment of seminaries for the formation of clergy in all the major cities of Spain, following the model of that which Saint Isidore had himself established in Seville.

At this stage, Isidore was well advanced in age. He foretold both his own impending death, as well as the invasion of Spain by the Saracens which was to occur in the near future. Having governed the Church in Seville for about forty years, he departed from this world into the Kingdom of Heaven in the Year of Our Lord 636.

In accordance with a request he made before his passing from this life, his body was interned between that of his [older] brother, Leander, and his [younger] sister, Florentina.

Translator's note

Both Leander, bishop of Seville, and Florentina, who was the abbess of a large convent of nuns, are venerated as saints. As previously noted, another brother of his, Fulgentius, bishop of Zaragoza, is also a saint.

Ferdinand I, King of Castile and León [who also was recognized as the Holy Roman Emperor, c. 1015–1065], obtained the mortal remains of Saint Isidore from Enetus, the Saracen governor who ruled Seville at the time, by paying to him a very great some of money. He reverently relocated the body of the saint to the city of León, where he had a magnificent basilica constructed and dedicated to him.[3] The relics of Saint Isidore are devoutly venerated in that holy temple to this day by the faithful, and innumerable miracles have occurred there through his holy intercession.

---

[3] The ancient Basilica of Saint Isidore, where the relics of the saint are located, remains as one of the major churches in the city of León at this present time.

A nineteenth-century representation of Saint Isidore of Seville with his brothers Saint Leandre and Saint Fulgence

AUTHOR'S INTRODUCTION:

The Mystical Significance and Hidden Teachings of Numbers in Sacred Scripture, and what Number Is

IT WILL BE by no means a superfluous or redundant undertaking to examine the meaning and significance of the various numbers which appear in the pages of Sacred Scripture. For these numbers are indeed full of hidden teachings and meanings, and contain within themselves a veritable richness of mystical signification. Hence, in response to various requests, I will undertake to set down in this work certain principles or rules for the understanding of the meaning of the numbers which are found in Sacred Scripture. I will endeavor to do this in a manner which is both brief and concise, yet sufficiently comprehensive and complete.

At the very beginning it is appropriate and useful to understand precisely what *number* is. Number is a gathering together or a congregation of multiple expressions or manifestations of a *unity*. From this initial unity proceeds all other numbers, even unto the greatest multitude. There is, potentially, no final ending to this progression of multitudes or numbers, which could be extended indefinitely. The conclusion of it would be the *All,* or the entire universe. But this *All,* or everything which exists, even if it were to be extended to infinity, would all necessarily proceed from the initial *One* or primal Unity.

An even number is one which is able to be divided into two equal parts, while an odd number is one which cannot be divided into two equal parts. If you attempt to divide an odd number of anything into two equal parts, you will find that you are either one short of having the parts equal, or that there is one left over. In another sense, the term *even* can be used to describe the series of numbers in which each number can be divided into two equal parts, and then these two equal parts can also be divided equally, and so on, until one arrives at unity. An example of this would be 64. Half of 64 is 32; and half of 32 is 16; half of 16 is eight, and half of eight is four. Half of four is two; and half of two is one, or unity.

Translator's note

This series of numbers produced by successive doubling which Saint Isidore has just described (1, 2, 4, 8, 16, 32, etc.) is now known as a 'geometric sequence,' employing a ratio of two. In his time, the term 'even number' (in Latin, 'numerus par') was sometimes applied to the numbers of this sequence, as well as being applied (more commonly) to the series of what are now called 'even numbers.'

UNITY, OR ONE

ONE IS THE smallest of the numbers, which is not able to be divided further into any other whole number. Technically, unity or *one* is not really a number at all, since if there is only one of something, it cannot truly be said that there is 'a number' of that thing. But one or unity is the seed and basis of all subsequent numbers.

For out of unity, all subsequent numbers emanate or are created. For this reason, a unity or *unit* is the necessary measure of anything. Additions of units are the cause of all *increase,* while numbers of units are also the means of identifying or enumerating *decreases.* For all increases in number arise from the additions of a unit, or a series or collections of units. Similarly, if units are progressively taken from any number, eventually you will arrive at *one,* or a unit or unity.

For example, if there is ten of something, this number will not be increased unless a unit, or a succession or collection of units, is added to that ten. And if you remove units from that ten successively, you will eventually arrive at one, or a unity.

A unit is, by its very nature, indivisible, insofar as it is a unit. And a unit, insofar as it is a unit, is necessarily also complete in itself.

Translator's note

Although Saint Isidore does not speak here of fractions, the mathematical and practical possibilities of fractions does not contradict what he says. For example, if one whole is divided into two the result is one half, and if that one half is divided in two, the result is one quarter. 'One whole', insofar as it is and remains 'one whole,' cannot be divided. And, to qualify as 'one whole,' it is necessarily complete in itself.

The most perfect example of unity is God Himself, who is the fundamental unity from which all that exists is generated and made possible. And there is one Mediator between God and man, indivisible and complete in Himself, the man Jesus Christ. The Holy Spirit, the Paraclete, is also one.

Translator's note

Saint Isidore here demonstrates that the doctrine of the Holy Trinity does not contradict the unity of God, for this unity (which is, by its nature, only one and the same) exists in and is essential to Father, Son, and Holy Spirit.

The Holy Mother Church is also defined and identified as one. That unity or oneness is an essential element of the Holy Church is symbolically revealed in the fact that when the prophet Ezekiel witnessed in a vision the threshold of the temple in the new Jerusalem being measured, it was one rod in length.

Translator's note

The vision referred to here is found in Ezekiel 40:1–8. The relevant passage, which highlights symbolically the essential nature of unity to the Church, is reproduced below:

> *In the visions of God, [the angel of the Lord] brought me into the land of Israel, and set me upon a very high mountain: upon which there was a building like a great city, bending towards the south. And he brought me in there, and behold a man, whose appearance was like the appearance of brass, with a line of flax in his hand, and a measuring reed in his hand, and he stood in the gate [. . .] and he measured the breadth of the temple. It was one length, and the height was one reed. And he came to the gate that looked toward the east, and he went up the steps thereof: and he measured the breadth of the threshold of the gate. And it was one reed, that is, one threshold was one reed broad. [. . .] And every little chamber was one reed long, and one*

> *reed broad. (...) And the threshold of the gate by the porch of the gate within, was one reed.*

This symbolism of the essential unity of the Church is also expressed in the ark of Noah. For when the Lord instructs Noah on the measurements of the ark, He says: "And in one cubit you shall finish it above."[1] Noah is also told that there should be one single door to this ark—also symbolizing the essential unity of the Church, which is truly the ark of our salvation. For, as Saint Paul tell us, there is one baptism, by which admission to the Church is conferred, and likewise there is one single faith which is everywhere and at all times professed within the one Church of God.[2]

The universe (by its very nature as a *universe*, which, by definition, contains all that there is in creation) is also one. And when we perceive the one sun, it produces but one light. It is on account of this reality that wise philosophers have always grasped the fundamental unity of the world or universe. For it exists and functions in an underlying harmony or concord, whereby all the parts and actions are bound together as one by a kind of affinity, co-operation or friendship. And all the parts and actions of the universe are mutually connected (even if these connections are not

---

1 Gen. 6:16.
2 See Ephesians 4:5.

always immediately perceptible), such that, viewed as a whole, it operates as a single, united system or cosmos.

A unity is thus that which cannot be divided, for, wherever there is one, it must be a totality in itself. An example of this indivisibility is apparent if we consider a geometrical straight line. Now, such a line cannot be divided along its width or breadth, because a line, in geometry, is understood as having no breadth, but only length. If it had breadth, it would not be a line, but a plane.

The number one thus represents both indivisibility and completeness, both of which, as has been noted, find their perfect exemplar and archetype in the one God Himself. The unity of God is of a special and particular variety, which pertains to God alone.[3] For it is the single primal and ultimate Unity. For God is in all things, and before all things, and beyond all things. He is one, and His attributes (including omnipotence, magnificence, and incomprehensibility) are also one, since they exist in indivisible unity and completeness. Hence Sacred Scripture declares emphatically this divine unity to be the very essence of God, and the essence of God to be supreme unity: "Hear, O Israel, the Lord your God is One."

---

[3] From this point until the end of the present chapter, text from the *Libellus de Numeris* (*Small book on numbers*), also attributed to Saint Isidore, has been incorporated (PL LXXXIII:1293–1302). It continues his meditations and reflections on the nature of unity, and in particular, the essential unity of both God and man.

Who or what indeed is there in Heaven or on earth or under the earth which is similar or comparable to God—in power, in Trinity, in Unity, in divinity, in perfection of humanity? And therefore God is the "One and only," for neither before, nor after, nor now, nor then, is anything or anyone who could be compared to Him. For the devil, who, in pride, dared to liken or compare himself to God (and thereby challenged the uniqueness or oneness of the Deity), was immediately cast down, and became instead the first among the creatures of hell.

Translator's note

The third- and fourth-century Pythagorean philosopher Iamblichus expresses the divine nature of unity beautifully and eloquently, in the somewhat similar terms to those used by Isidore:[4]

> *All things have been ordered by Unity, because it contains everything potentially. [. . .] And God coincides with this primal Unity, since He is the origin of everything which exists, just as Unity is in the case of number. Unity is the beginning, middle and end of all quantity, of all size, and of every other quality. And just as without Unity there can be no subsistence or existence of anything at all, so also without it there is no possible knowledge of anything. For it is a pure light, supreme over all that exists, and it is sun-like and Monarch of*

[4] Iamblichus, *The Theology of Arithmetic,* 1.

all the universe. Thus in each of these respects, Unity bears the image of the nature of God Himself.

Among the creations of God, there are certain things which, though there are many individual instances of them, are still described as being "one," reflecting their indivisibility and completeness. Speaking in this way, it is said: "Man is one," or "The soul is one." Similarly, we say "one faith,"[5] "one baptism,"[6] "one love," "one hope,"[7] "one faith," "one peace," "one chalice," and "one bread."[8]

We shall speak now of some of these examples, as God grants us, showing why they are mystically said to be "one," although they do not consist of single instances, but rather many or several.

To begin with man, in the beginning we discover the God created one man. And from the rib of this single man, Adam, one woman, Eve, was formed. And all humanity spoke one language, until the time of the Tower of Babel.

We are said to have one, single father to our faith, Abraham, and from Adam until the time of Christ, there was no other man who had this particular name. Of him it was said: "Abraham believed in God, and it was counted unto him as righteousness."[9] But did not Abel also believe in

---

5 Eph. 4:5.
6 Eph. 4:5.
7 Eph. 1:4.
8 1 Cor. 1:17.
9 Gen. 15:16; Rom. 4:3; Jas. 2:23.

God, and receive the crown of martyrdom? Did not Enoch also believe in God, who was taken up by the Lord while still alive in the body? Was not Noah, who was counted as righteous, a believer in God, for the Lord instructed him to build the ark and liberated him and those with him by means of it? But neither Abel nor Enoch nor Noah are described as being "our father in faith?" The reason is that, although there were isolated individuals who believed in God, it was only since the time of Abraham that such faith was maintained with continuity and unity. To represent the indivisibility and completeness of this faith in the One God, it is described as having one founder or father, namely Abraham.

Next, we may consider in what sense man, who is created in the image and likeness of the God who is supremely One, is also truly said to be "one."

Translator's note

This oneness of man is represented in the singular person of Adam created by God, and also in the fact that "man" in the singular is used to speak of all human beings in general, e.g., "Man does not live of bread alone." The term 'individual' literally means 'indivisible,' and each human being is necessarily a complete entity. Thus, the oneness of the human being is held to be a reflection of the transcendent unity of the Deity. This perspective imparts a deep mystical significance to Christ's prayer: "May they all may be one; as thou, Father, are Me, and I in Thee, may they also may be One in us,"[10] *which could equally be rendered as "May each one of them be one . . ."*

Man is formed from two substances, the soul and the body, but these two substances are so intimately and necessarily conjoined that together they form a single entity, the human being. In each of the two elements of which this human entity is formed, it is possible to detect or to describe multiple aspect. For example, in the body of a human being, there are seen, without the least doubt, to be nine elements. There are the four physical elements—namely, earth, water, air, and fire. Out of these are found the subsequent five varieties which are generated therefrom—namely, salt, grass, flowers, stones, and clouds. So that you may perceive this more readily, read carefully what follows. In the mass of the body is the *earth*; the element of *water* forms sweat and saliva; *air* is the substance of the breath; while *fire* is manifested in the warmth of the blood and the capacity of the digestion to 'cook' further the food it receives. *Salt* is present in the saltiness of blood, sweat, and tears. *Grass* is manifested in the hairs of the head and the body; while *flowers* are exhibited in the variety of colors of the eyes. *Stones* are present in the hardness and density of bones, and it is indeed fitting that stones are sometimes referred to as 'the bones of the earth.' Finally, the fluid and nebulous quality of *clouds* is

[10] Jn. 17:21.

revealed in the fluctuating and ever-mobile thoughts, cogitations and emotions of the mind.

And to these nine substances (the four basic physical elements, and the five growths which emerge from these), the human body also includes the joints of the bones, the principal of which number no less than 365. And the number of small joints and connections is virtually countless. The principal veins of the body are likewise 365, with numberless minor veins and capillaries. And this is not to mention vast multitude of the nerves and hairs, and so forth.

Thus the human body is truly a microcosmos, or a small universe. Like the macrocosm, or greater universe, it is fundamentally and essentially one, despite the virtually infinite multitude of its constituent elements, for it is complete and integrated as a single harmonious unit, as the apostle Saint Paul teaches us.[11]

The soul is the other of the two principal constitutive substances of the human person. What exactly is this soul, we may wonder? Does it live, or not? And if it lives, is its life one of blessedness or of misery? What, therefore, is the soul?

The soul is neither of the Heavens nor of the earth; nor is it of air, fire or water. It is not itself God, nor is it generated by the soul of either the father or the mother. It is neither seen, nor heard, nor smelt, nor tasted. Hence this

---

[11] See 1 Corinthians 12:12–27.

mysterious and otherwise inexplicable force of life is given directly by God Himself, and created *ex nihilo*; for it can be explained in no other way. Scripture testifies to the fact that the soul, which is the force of life itself, is a direct creative emanation or gift of God, when the Lord declares through the prophet Isaiah: "My Spirit shall go forth from me, and I have created all breath,"[12] that is, every soul.

The soul is the rational and sensible life force, spiritually imparting vitality, and, at the command of the Creator, invisibly and miraculously causing all the members of the body, both internal and external, to live and move, for without the soul the body would be inanimate. The principal functions of the soul are sensing, exercising judgment on that which is perceived, and thinking or reflecting, and willing or desiring. When each of these functions operate well, then the image of God within the human being actively lives; and when they operate both well and virtuously in a manner that is pleasing to God and His angels, then it becomes, in its action and operation, a true throne of the Holy Trinity.

O Reader, whoever you are, you are a union of the body and soul and it behooves you to emulate the supreme Unity of God, made flesh in Christ, and reflected also in the saints. Learn from Christ, humility; from Saint Peter, devotion; from Saint John, love; from Abraham, obedience;

---

[12] Is. 57:16.

from Lot, hospitality; from Isaac, patience; from Job, endurance; from Saint Joseph, chastity; and from Saint Mary Magdalene, true sorrow for sin. For these virtues and all others, though seemingly many, are inseparably united in God, whose attributes are all indivisible. And this glorious and divine unity is reflected in the virtues and character of each of the saints.

TWO

THE NUMBER TWO is, properly speaking, the first number, since one is technically not a number at all, as explained at the beginning of the previous chapter. It is the first number to be generated from unity, and the expression of a relationship of connection or likeness of nature, and so the fundamental beginning of all motion and of all relationship and interaction. It expresses and reflects relationships and connections of commensurability or comparability, such as the bond of friendship between one human being and another, or the bond of fraternity of a man with his brother.

Translator's note

This commensurability or comparability does not necessarily imply equality. However, for two things to be identified as 'two of something', they need first to be placed within the same category. For example, a pair of human beings and a pair of trees would be described as 'two trees' or 'two human beings' respectively. But a tree and a human being together would not generally be counted as being 'two,' unless the category by which they were identified and counted as was so broad as to include both, e.g., 'two erect vertical objects.'

Yet while the number two symbolizes a relationship of affinity or likeness (such that the persons, object, or items can be meaningfully counted together to be described as two of something), it is also the first number which is capable of division. Thus, it simultaneously represents the possibility of fundamental opposition, and signifies the primary dualities which give rise to the possibility of conflict. This fundamental duality, or the possibility of opposition between binaries, is found in the dichotomy of good and evil, light and darkness, life and death, and many other binary pairings. Where two items or persons are contrasted with each other, the number two represents both a comparability of kind or nature, but also conflict or divergence in respect to character. There are many such examples of this in Scripture, such as the two baskets of figs—one of fine figs and the other of poor figs—which were revealed to the prophet Jeremiah in a vision.[13]

Translator's note

In connection with this symbolism of two as representing the twofold potential within human nature for either good or evil

---

13 See Jer. 24:4–7.

(and the freedom of the choice between the two), conflicting or contrasting pairings of brothers seem to be particularly significant. Examples of this include Cain and Abel,[14] *Ishmael and Isaac,*[15] *and Jacob and Esau.*[16] *To these may be added the pairings of brothers with contrasting behaviors used as illustrations in the teachings of Our Lord, such as in the parable of the prodigal son,*[17] *or in the parable of the two sons, one of which did the will of his father while the other did not.*[18]

So it is that the number of two, while representing likeness of nature and therefore affinity and potential union, also represents symbolically the potential for division from such a unity or union and conflict. This number of two is represented in the command to Noah to bring each species onto his ark in pairs of male and female, and here it mystically foreshadows the tendencies both to union and division which are manifested within the universe.

Translator's note

The Latin text of Genesis 7:2, in which the number of each species to be taken into the ark, is somewhat ambiguous, yet seems to indicate seven pairs of each clean animal, and two pairs of each unclean animal. The fact that pairs (i.e., groupings of two) are meant is indicated in the specification that,

---

[14] See Gen. 4:1–16.
[15] See Gen. 21:1–21.
[16] See Gen. 25.
[17] See Luke 15:11–32.
[18] See Matthew 21:28–32.

whether clean or unclean, each numbering is to include both male and female

The symbolism of division is represented again symbolically in the specification in the Gospel passage which speaks of two persons being in a field, of which one will be left while the other will be taken away at the end of the age.[19] This pertains to persistence or perseverance in faith in virtue, and expresses the possibility of either adherence to faith in times of tribulation and temptation or the possibility of falling away when confronted with difficulties and challenges.

The number two, considering its other significance as that of union or likeness, mystically represents also concordance in good and concordance through the good. An expression of this is found in the division of Sacred Scripture itself into the Old Testament (the Law) and the New Testament (the Gospel), which together harmoniously reveal the will of God and His plan for salvation.

The same mystical symbolism of two as harmony and convergence in and through the good is exhibited in the two stone tables upon which the Law of God was written, as revealed to Moses.[20]

This harmony or union is likewise expressed in the two trumpets of silver which God instructs Moses to have fashioned: "Make for yourself two trumpets of silver, of

---

19 See Matthew 24:40.

20 See Exodus 31:18 and 34:1.

hammered work you shall make; and you shall use them for summoning the congregation and for having the camps advance forth."[21] These two trumpets, which represent the means by which people are summoned to salvation, express the twin saving elements of the Law and grace.

We are told also of the two six-winged seraphim, who sit before the throne of God, and who zealously pour forth hymns of glory, ceaselessly proclaiming:

"Holy, holy, holy, Lord God of Hosts;
All the earth is full of His glory."[22]

Translator's note

The threefold "Holy" in the songs of these two seraphim is, of course, traditionally understood to be a reflection of the Trinitarian nature of God, and an expression of the mystery of the Trinity. The six wings of the two seraphim are the result of a multiplication by two (i.e., the two seraphim harmonizing in son) of this sacred number three.

In the book of the prophet Zechariah, we encounter likewise two olive trees which are seen in the vision of the prophet, one to the left and one to the right of the golden candelabrum, which bears seven lamps with seven lights. These two olive trees symbolize the convergence of varied paths to the illuminating truth of God, namely those of the

---

[21] Num. 10:1–2.
[22] See Isaias 6:1–3.

Old and New Testaments, and the convergence or harmony of the Law and of grace.

Translator's note

The passage in question is found in Zechariah 4:2–3, and reads thus:

> *And [the angel] spoke to me, saying: "What do you see?" And I said: "I have looked, and, behold, a candelabrum all of gold, and its lamp upon the top of it: and it had seven lights upon it, and seven funnels for the lights that were upon the top of it. There were two olive trees over it: one upon the right side of the lamp, and the other upon the left side."*

The number two occurs also very prominently in the Songs of Songs, where it represents the union of the Lover and the Beloved, as well as the desire for this union. The text speaks frequently of the two breasts of the Bridegroom, comparing them with two twin roes or young deer which graze among the lilies.[23] The bride here is understood as representing the Church, longing for and seeking union with Christ, who is the divine Bridegroom.

In the Apocalypse, two witnesses are commanded to prophesy.[24] Similarly, in the Gospel when the seventy-two

---

23 See Canticle of Canticles 4:5.

24 See Revelation 11:3. In Revelation 11:4, these two witnesses are identified with two olive trees, creating a link with the vision of Zechariah 4:2–3, previously cited.

disciples are sent forth to proclaim the Word of the Lord, they are sent out in pairs (i.e., two by two), providing again the requisite two witnesses.[25] For the pairing of two witnesses, whose evidence is in concord, serves to establish, both symbolically and literally, the veracity of whatever it is to which they testify.

Our Lord declares that both the Law and the prophets (a pairing which expresses unity), are expressed in their totality in the two precepts of love of God and love of neighbor, which are described as being like each other.[26] And the precept of love of neighbor is not fulfilled or possible except where society or community exists in some form—which only comes into being when there are at least two human beings in interaction. And some form of society or community exists whenever and wherever two human beings are placed in connection or interaction with each other. The number two therefore represents here the essential and constitutive element of true society or community, namely charity and justice.

Finally, there are two aspects or means which lead a human being to blessedness of life—namely, faith and good works. Faith is a grace or the gift of the divinity, while good works proceed from a right manner of living on the part of the human being concerned. And the Church affirms

25 See Luke 23:1.
26 See Matthew 22:37–40, Mark 12: 30–21; and Luke 10:27.

there to be two lives of man, the temporal life or the life of this world, and the eternal life or hereafter for which we are destined. In the first form of life, we live by faith, perceiving God only "through a glass and darkly";[27] whereas in the second, we shall rejoice forever in the contemplation of God in the fulness of complete understanding.

---

[27] 1 Cor. 13:12.

THREE

THREE IS THE first of the odd or uneven numbers,[28] and it represents perfection. For this number, in its three components, possesses a beginning (the first unit), a middle (the second unit), and an end (the third unit). These three elements (the beginning, middle, and end), are united in a manner of perfect equality.[29] And those there are these three constitutive units which together form a perfect whole, they are nevertheless perfectly one, as the number three of the Trinity of Triad. This reflects the mystery of the God, in which there is one Divinity, yet a distinction of three Persons, in each of whom the Unity of the Godhead

[28] Note that Isidore does not classify one as being technically a number at all, hence three is the first odd number.

[29] This same insight is offered by the Pythagorean philosopher, Nichomachus of Gerasa, in his deeply influential *Theology of Arithmetic*, cited in the work of the same title by Iamblichus: "The Trinity or Triad is the first number which is simultaneous beginning, middle and end within itself, and these elements are the causes and completion of all perfection. Thus, the Trinity is the form of perfection of all things." Iamblichus, *Theology of Arithmetic*, 3.

is fully present. In nature or substance (*ousia*) it is one, but in appellation or identification (or in *hypostatis*) it is three.

Very rightly, the number three, therefore, should be grasped as reflecting or manifesting the nature of the Holy Trinity. And it is always by this number that the divinity is proclaimed throughout the world. And it is similarly this number of three which is used by the angelic host of Heaven to hail and acclaim God. For they chant without ceasing the eternal hymn of the *Trisagion,* or the 'Thrice-Holy', resounding to the glorious strains of: "Holy, Holy, Holy!"

Translator's note

This observation shows the fact that the doctrine of the Trinity is universal to all heterodox forms of Christianity. But it also reflects Saint Isidore's detailed knowledge of the use of a Trinity to represent Divinity in other philosophical and religious traditions of the world, and not only Christianity. In neo-Platonism (which strongly influenced early Christianity), God was understood to be a unity of the Monad (or the One), the Intellect, and the Soul. In Hinduism, the one supreme Deity (Brahman) was understood as being manifested in three divine forms or as three divine persons, Brahma (the Creator), Vishnu (the Preserver), and Shiva (the Judge). Similar Triune understandings of God are also to be found in many other traditions. This does not mean, of course, the Christianity 'borrowed' its Trinitarian doctrine from elsewhere in any sense, but rather that the Triune nature of God is supported by reason itself.

The ark of Noah was constructed with three chambers or levels, and out of these three chambers the entire human race was regenerated after the flood. The height of the ark was thirty cubits (i.e., three times ten), while its length was three hundred cubits (i.e., three times a hundred).[30] And other examples of the number three as being connected with salvation from God abound throughout the Scriptures.

The number of three, mystically representing the Trinity and the perfection of God Himself, appears with this symbolism in the venerable pages of the histories of the patriarchs. Thus it was that three angels visited Abraham, which were certainly an image of the Holy Trinity, for he greeted them as 'Lord,' using the singular form of address.[31] Isaac opened three wells in the earth, which the Philistines had previously stopped up.[32] Jacob placed three rods or branches (from poplar, almond, and plane trees) in the waters from which the flocks which he tended drank.[33] The prophet Jonah remained in the belly of the whale for some three days;[34] and it was for three days that, in response to the preaching of Jonah, the citizens of Nineveh fasted and undertook penance to mitigate the wrath of God.[35]

---

30 See Genesis 6:15.
31 See Genesis 8:1–18.
32 See Genesis 18:26.
33 See Genesis 30:37.
34 See Jonas 1:17.
35 See Jonas 3.

In the Gospel, also, the number of three, representing perfection, abounds. For example, Lazarus remains in the tomb for three days, representing the completeness of his death, and is raised to life only on the fourth day.[36] Likewise, the parable of the woman hiding the yeast within the flour to cause it all to be leavened specifies that it was three measures of flour in which it was hidden.[37]

It was three times that God[38] prayed that the chalice of the passion should pass Him by.[39] And it was three times that Saint Peter denied Christ, and similarly three times that he affirmed that he loved Him. After His death, the Redeemer remained buried in the tomb for three days. And it was three times that He is recorded in the Gospel to have revealed Himself to His disciples after the Resurrection.

Similarly, there are three theological virtues which are commended by God through the writings of the apostle Saint Paul—faith, hope, and love. In these three virtues, all power of prophecy and holy insight consists. And there are three forms or levels of fruitfulness which are identified in the Gospel—the hundredfold, the sixty-fold, and the thirty-fold.[40] The hundredfold fruitfulness represents that

[36] See John 11.
[37] See Matthew 13:33 and Luke 13:20–21.
[38] Very interestingly, in the Latin text Isidore uses the term "*Deus*" here, rather than the more expected "*Christus,*" and this choice is retained in the present translation.
[39] See Matthew 26:26–46.
[40] See Mathew 13:8.

of the martyrs; the sixty-fold fruitfulness symbolizes that of holy persons who consecrate themselves to celibacy or virginity for God; while the thirty-fold fruitfulness is manifested in the virtue of holy married persons.

There are three essential properties, characteristic of all things within the created universe, which God Himself and God alone entirely transcends. These three properties are measure, place, and time. There are also three movements or actions of which the human soul is capable—namely desire, wrath, and reason. And there are three languages in which the mysteries of the sacred law are written, and these same three languages were used on the inscription upon the cross of Christ—Hebrew, Greek, and Latin.[41]

There are to be found three senses of the intelligence or human understanding—historical (or literal), moral, and mystical. Hence it is that Sacred Scripture can be interpreted according to each of these senses.[42] The philosophers, following the same three senses, likewise declare that there are three principal fields of wisdom and knowledge—physical, which pertains to the historical or literal sense; ethical, which pertains to the moral sense; and logical or abstract, which pertains to the mystical.

---

[41] See John 19:20.

[42] Later traditions typically identify *four* senses of Scripture—literal (or historical), allegorical, moral (or tropological), and anagogical. However, Isidore is here apparently combining the allegorical and anagogical senses into what he calls the mystical sense.

There are three techniques or procedures whereby musical sounds may be produced. These are by using the voice directly, by breathing into an instrument, and finally by striking something (either a string or an object). The voice is used by singers, breathing into a vessel is used by flautist, and the procedure of striking is used by harpists and performers upon the lyre as well as by players of percussion instruments.

There are three forms of rational creatures in the universe: the angels in Heaven, human beings upon the earth; and demons in the underworld. And the history of the world, in terms of salvation, may be divided into three eras or epochs: the time preceding the law (from Adam until Moses), the time of the law (from Moses until Christ), and finally the time of grace (from Christ onwards). And the world is divided geographically into three principal regions—namely Europe, Asia, and Libya.[43]

Each of the seasons of the year (spring, summer, autumn, and winter) consist of three months. And finally, the testimony of three witnesses is universally agreed to be evidence of the truth of their testimony, and puts an end to any uncertainty.[44]

---

[43] This statement reflects the knowledge of the world at the time of Isidore. 'Libya' should be understood here as referring to the entire continent of Africa.

[44] See Deuteronomy 19:15; Matthew 18:16; 1 John 5:8.

So it is that not only the pages of Sacred Scripture, but the organization and structure of the world and universe itself, are replete with the number three—representing completion, plenitude, and perfection. In this way, the Triune nature of the true God is witnessed, reflected, and glorified.

FOUR

WHAT SHALL I say of the marvels of the number of four, in which stability and solidity is expressed with such perfection and clarity? The first four number together united form the *decade* or ten: for one, plus two, plus three, plus four equals ten. This decade is understood as representing complete fullness and solidity, and partaking in or expressing unity or the One, and this completion or fullness is contained and mystically expressed completely in the number four.

Likewise, a hundred is formed from the first four decades added together: ten, plus twenty, plus thirty, plus forty gives one hundred, a complete century. And the same pattern is to be found in respect to 1,000 (100 + 200 + 300 + 400 = 1,000), and 10,000, and all other such complete quantities, which are magnifications of the unity.

Translator's note

Saint Isidore is describing what was known in the ancient world as the 'sacred decad' or Tetractys or Tetrad. It was the number ten, understood or conceived as the sum of the numbers one, two, three and four. This was believed to be of particular mystical and cosmic significance to followers of the philosophy or Pythagoras, and was an important subject of meditation for them. The four components of Tetractys were believed also to correspond to the four elements, four cardinal directions (north, south, east, and west), the four seasons, etc., and so this Tetractys (or Tetrad) was held to represent the completion of the universe, or the multitude understood as a unity.

The Tetractys is represented graphically by an equilateral triangle constructed from ten points, of which the apex is one point, the second from the top is two points, the third level from the top is three points, and the fourth level from the top (the lowest level) is four points, as shown below:

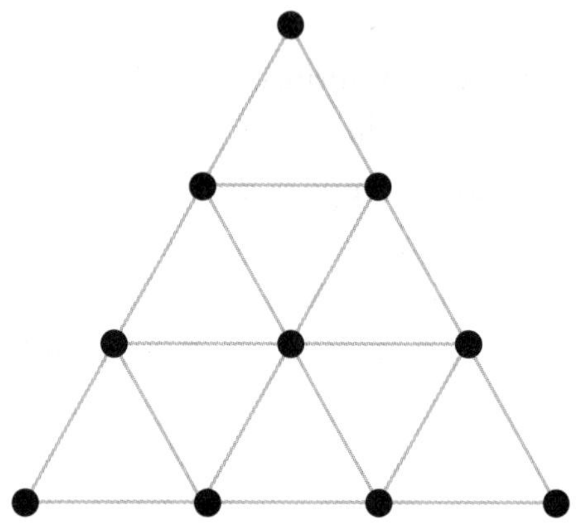

This formation, which (as an equilateral triangle) is also Trinitarian, was believed to be of great and profound mystical significance. To this day, it is depicted in the tassels on either side of an archbishop's coat of art.

*In connection with the sacred and divine nature of the number four, highlighted in the Tetractys of the Pythagoreans, the importance of the Tetragrammaton (*יהוה*), or four-letter name of God whose meaning is "I am who am," should be noted. This Tetragrammaton is also often depicted in the triangular form the 'sacred decad,' as shown below:*

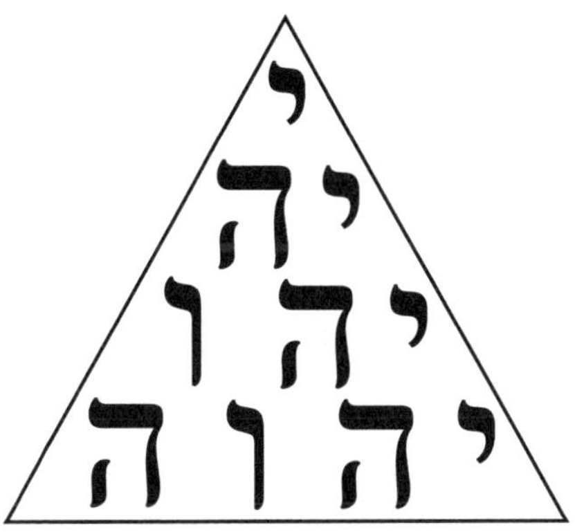

The number four is represented particularly in the four canonical Gospels. This number is deeply significant here, for it represents the fact that the Gospel is to be proclaimed throughout all the corners or regions of the world—to the north, the south, the east, and the west. This same reality is represented also in the four rivers which flowed from paradise; Pishon, Gihon, the Tigris, and the Euphrates.[45] The ark of Noah was constructed from planks of wood, each having four sides.[46] In the Old Law, it is specified that the sacred vestments are to be of four colors—being sown of gold, and blue, purple and scarlet yarn.[47]

In a vision of the prophet Ezekiel, when he witnesses the dry bones in a valley to take flesh and become animated, it is specified that it is four winds (or spirits) which restores them to life. This restoration of the dry bones to life is, of course, a mystical pre-figuring of the future Resurrection. In the book of the prophet Daniel, the prophet describes his vision of four winds from Heaven, which strove or battled upon a great sea. This sea represents here the world, while the four winds are angelic powers. These four winds from Heaven also symbolize the four Gospels, extended throughout the expanse of the world.

In the same vision, Daniel also witnessed four beasts, representing the four kingdoms or empires of the world.[48]

The prophet Zechariah likewise speaks of four craftsmen or carpenters, whom he witnessed breaking down the four horns which had scattered the people of Israel. Again, these four craftsmen represent the four Evangelists, and their

---

45 See Genesis 2:10–14. The River Gihon is believed to be the Nile.

46 See Genesis 6:14. The Vulgate records God as instructed Noah to build this wood from "*lignis laevigates*," which is rendered as "wooden planks" in the Douay-Reims version.

47 See Genesis 28:1–5.

48 See Daniel 7.

Gospel which goes forth into the four cardinal directions (north, south, east, and west) of the Heavens, and likewise into the four regions of the world, which represent its totality. In the Apocalypse, Saint John beholds four living creatures—one having the countenance of a lion, one of an ox, one of a man, and one of an eagle.[49] Each of these living creatures again depicts one of the Evangelists. And these four creatures each have six wings.[50] The total number of wings is thus 24, corresponding with the number of elders before the throne of God.[51] These four creatures again represent the entirety of the earth (north, south, east, and west), and the four cardinal directions or faces of the Heavens.

The physical universe itself is formed from four elements—namely fire, air, water, and earth. And the year progresses through four distinct seasons—summer, autumn, winter, and spring. And the human body is animated or suffused with four qualities or humors—heat, coldness, wetness, and dryness. There are four virtues which the human soul may possess; justice, prudence, fortitude, and temperance. And in opposition to these four virtues of the soul there are four vices; cupidity, fear, despair or lethargy, and exultation or elation.

---

[49] See Revelation 4:6–8. Traditionally, the creature with the human face is believed to correspond with Matthew, while the lion corresponds with Mark, the ox corresponds with Luke, and the eagle corresponds with John.

[50] See Revelation 4:8.

[51] See Revelation 4:4.

Translator's note

The four 'virtues which the soul may possess' referred to here are the traditional four 'cardinal virtues.' These were strengths or qualities of mind or soul, identified since the time of the classical philosophers, and consisted of prudence, justice, fortitude, and temperance. They are identified by both Plato and Aristotle, and also appear in Sacred Scripture the book of the Wisdom of Solomon[52] *and in the non-canonical fourth book of Maccabees.*[53] *See also Aquinas,* Summa Theologica, *II(I).61.*

All mortal life itself comprises four essential stages or events—a beginning or time of initial formation or conception, a period of growth and development, then a period of stasis or remaining in completed maturity, and finally a period of decline. And there are four genres of living creatures which occupy the universe—celestial beings or angels; the winged creatures which fly in the skies above the earth; the aquatic creatures of the oceans, lakes, and rivers; and the terrestrial animals which walk or crawl upon the earth.

The rainbow exhibits in the Heavens a four-colored splendor, deriving these from the four elements themselves.

Translator's note

In Medieval times, it was believed that the rainbow exhibited four colors. In his Etymology, Isidore writes: "The rainbow is

[52] See Wisdom 8:7.
[53] See 4 Maccabees 1:18–19.

of four colors, and takes its appearance from all of the elements into itself. From the sky it draws red, which is the color of the element of fire; from the element of water it derives the color of purple; from the element of air, it takes the color of white; and finally from the element of earth it gathers the color black."[54] *Of course, the numbering of colors in a rainbow is primarily a matter of nomenclature.*

Finally, every four years, a leap year or intercalary year is calculated to occur, indicating that this is the completion of cycle or period.

Translator's note

This idea that each four years form together a complete unit or cycle is reflected also in the notion of the Olympiad, or four-year period, corresponding with the eponymous festival of games. The use of Olympiads to identify times was used not only in the ancient world, but also continued in Medieval Europe, by which time the ancient Olympic Games of Greece had long since fallen into abeyance.

Thus it is that the number four, whenever it is encountered in Sacred Scripture, serves as a mystical symbol of the fullness and entirety of the universe, and the all-embracing totality of the Gospel of salvation.

---

[54] *Libri Etymologiarum,* XIII:1.

FIVE

NEXT FOLLOWS THE number five. This number has a unique property, that whenever it is multiplied either by itself or by any other odd number, it always produces a numeral concluding with the digit five.[55] Thus five time five produces 25 (XXV); three times five produces 15 (XV); seven times five produces 35 (XXXV); and nine times five produces 45 (XLV). Thus when five is a factor multiplied with any other number which is congruent with it in genus (i.e., with any other odd number), it always manifests its presence and nature clearly and visibly. For this reason, the number five is mystically emblematic of the Law of God, and this Law is manifested in a five-fold manner, signifying that its proper and congruent expressions will always be in accordance clearly and visibly, although they may vary in

[55] Although Roman, rather than Arabic numbers, were used in Isidore's time, this observation holds true for Roman numerals as well, as shown in the bracketed numbers given in the examples which follow.

their exact prescriptions and measures, as the quantities 15, 25, 35, etc., vary among themselves.

Thus it is mystically significant and very fitting that the ancient Law of the Hebrews was expressed and contained within the Pentateuch, or the five books of Moses. And the new commandment of Christ, which was especially dear to the beloved apostle Saint John, is expressed, not in five books, but in five simple words, which contain the whole essence of the law of God. And this New Commandment of five words, and the Law of God expressed in the five books of the Pentateuch, are (when properly understood and applied) always in harmony.

Translator's note

Despite the fact that Saint Isidor does not explicitly identify them, the words referred to here are clearly those of which Christ identifies as His New Commandment: "Diligatis invicem sicut dilexi vos"[56] *("Love one another, as I have loved you.") These five words are understood by the author as expressing the same principle as the Law of Moses, which was expressed in the five books of the Pentateuch or Torah.*

The specifications for the square altar in the book of Exodus state that it is to be five cubits in length and five cubits in width. And in the book of the prophet Isaiah, it is stated that there are five cities within the land of Egypt which

56 Jn. 13:34.

shall come to speak the language of the Canaanites (meaning the Hebrew language), and shall come to swear by the Lord of Hosts.

Translator's note

Isidore is referring here to the passage in Isaiah in which it is predicted that there will be five cities in Egypt which will come to faith in the true God, and to whom the future Savior will come. The passage in question (Isaiah 19:18–20), reads thus: "In that day there shall be five cities in the land of Egypt, speaking the language of Canaan, and swearing by the Lord of hosts: one shall be called the city of the sun. In that day there shall be an altar of the Lord in the midst of the land of Egypt, and a monument of the Lord at the borders thereof. It shall be for a sign, and for a testimony to the Lord of hosts in the land of Egypt. For they shall cry to the Lord because of the oppressor, and he shall send them a Savior and a defender to deliver them." This represents in an allegorical manner the going forth of the Gospel law to the pagan world, symbolized by Egypt. Egypt also represented symbolically the fields of philosophy and learning.

In the parable in the Gospel, we find that there are five wise virgins who appear, who are prepared for the arrival of their Lord; and also five foolish virgins, who do not have their lamps lighted.[57] And Christ fed a multitude

[57] See Matthew 25:1–13.

of people with bread from five loaves,[58] representing the nourishment which comes from the Word of God.[59]

The ancient philosophers stated that the globe of the world comprises five different zones.[60] And there are five vowels in the Latin alphabet. The senses of the human body are five—namely sight, hearing, smell, taste, and touch. And there are five varieties of animal upon the earth—namely human beings (or bipeds), quadrupeds, crawling animals, animals which swim in the waters, and animals which fly in the air.

Translator's note

Isidore's observation that the world is divided into five zones, that there are five vowels in the Latin language, that there are five senses, and that there are five different forms of animal on the earth (considered according to the mode of movement) seems to be related to his initial observation that the Law of God (both in the Pentateuch and the New Commandment) is expressed in the number five (the five books of Moses, or the five words of the New Commandment of Christ). For just as the number five remains identifiably and visibly harmonious

---

[58] See John 6:8–11.

[59] See Matthew 4:4.

[60] See Ovid, *Metamorphosis,* I:45–51. These five zones correspond with the modern global zonings, which divided the world into the North Frigid Zone, the North Temperate Zone, the Tropics, the South Frigid Zone, and the South Temperate Zone. Of these zones, Ovid and other philosophers in the ancient world held that only the Temperate Zones were suitable for human habitation, and the others were either too cold or excessively hot.

whenever multiplied by another number of a congruent nature (always producing a number concluding with the digit five), so the Law of God remains visibly harmonious whenever it is applied to, or 'filtered through,' varied particular circumstances or situations (represented by the five different zones, senses, etc.)

SIX

SIX IS A number which contains within itself a model of perfection or completeness. For if you take the first half of the series of numbers which lead to six (that is, one, two, and three), and add them together, they produce six. In fact, they do produce six regardless of whether they are added together, (1 + 2 + 3 + 4 = 6) or whether they are all multiplied together (1 x 2 x 3 = 6). There is no other number to be found in which this is the case, and thus six represents completeness in a special and particular way. This number, in being divided, is also thus fulfilled.

It was in six days that God performed His work of creation. On the first day, He created the firmament of Heaven; on the second day, light; on the third day, the sea and the dry land; on the fourth day, the stars; on the fifth day, the fish and the birds; and on the sixth day, the beasts of the earth and human beings.

There are six ages of the world, which corresponds to these six days of creation. The first of these ages is from Adam until Noah, the second is from Noah until Abraham, the third is from Abraham until David, the fourth is from David until the Babylonian exile, and the fifth was from the Babylonian exile until the time of Christ. The sixth age commenced from the time of Christ, and extends to this present day.

The number of days of the year is a reflection or magnification of the significance of the number six. For if you take sixty days, and multiply those sixty days by six, the result is 360 days. There are then five remaining days, but if you consider a leap year, there are, in fact, 366 days. On the other hand, every year technically consists not of 365 days, but 365 days plus a quarter of one day (i.e., six hours). And therefore the course of the year is contained within 366 days (that is [60 x 6] + 6 days), and the new year begins after six hours into the 366th day.

Translator's note

The learned editors of the Migne Patrologia Latina note that this observation is somewhat unclear or obscure in the original text. The present translation paraphrases it somewhat, hopefully making clear to the modern reader the intended sense of the author. The point made concerning the necessity of the leap year demonstrates that a year is not completed in 365 days, but rather in 365 days plus six hours, and therefore reaches its conclusion in the 366th day (i.e., [6 x 60] + 6 days.)

And if you take the number six and multiply it by four (which, as previously noted, is the number signifying firm solidity and completion), the result is 24, which is reflected in the 24 hours which form a day.

This linking of the number six with the completion of times is to be found most strikingly in the various stages of human life, which are six. The first of these stages is infancy, then childhood, then adolescence, then young adulthood, then maturity, and then finally old age. And all beings which exist may be divided into six classifications, which are ordered and hierarchical in nature. The first and lowest classification is inanimate objects, such as stones; the second is beings which are living, but which lack senses, such as plants and trees; the third is living things which possess senses, but are without rationality or reason, such as the beasts and birds; the fourth is creatures which are living, and which have senses, *and* which have reason, namely human beings. The fifth grade is those living creatures which have both senses and reason, and also are not subject to death—namely the angels of Heaven, together with the fallen spiritual beings which occupy hell. The sixth and highest grade of all is that unique and highest Being who alone is truly eternal, omnipotent and ever-blessed, who is God Himself and none other.

The number of properties or attributes, without which no object may exist in the physical universe, is six—for all objects must have: (1) size, (2) shape, (3) material or substance out of which they are formed, (4) position in space, (5) duration in time, and (6) movement. Also, there are six different possibilities for movement for any object—forwards, backwards, to the left, to the right, upwards, or downwards.

Many examples of the symbolic importance of the number six are to be found in Sacred Scripture. For it was on the sixth day that human beings were created in the image of God, and it was in the sixth age of man that the Savior appeared in the world in human flesh. Likewise, it was on the sixth day that the Israelites in the desert were commanded to gather a double ration of manna for their sustenance in the desert.[61]

In the book of the prophet Ezekiel, we find that the prophet perceived in a vision a man holding a measuring rod which was six cubits in length, and he is then led through six gates into the temple.[62] And, in the same vision,

---

61 See Exodus 16:22.
62 See Ezechiel 40:6–46.

Ezekiel receives the command that the prince is to offer six lambs in sacrifice.[63]

Six were the number of stone vessels of water which Our Lord transformed into wine in His first sign or miracle at the wedding feast at Cana.[64] And it was six days before the Passover that Christ entered into the city of Jerusalem in triumph.

There are a great many other examples, yet I shall not list them all, lest I exhaust my reader's attention at this point.

---

[63] See Ezechiel 46:6.

[64] See John 2:1–11.

SEVEN

IT MAY BE said of the number seven that it is not begotten or generated. Neither, within the series of the first ten numbers, does it generate another. For seven cannot be produced by multiplying any of the numbers which have proceeded it together. And it, in turn, cannot be multiplied with any number to produce any another number within the first ten. In this respect, seven is unique amongst all the first ten numbers, and stands out because of this as self-sufficient and pure, not being the product of any other number, nor generating any other number out of the first ten. In this respect, it expresses or symbolized the unique and uncreated nature of God Himself.

Translator's note

Isidore's observation here is indeed readily found to be accurate. For four, six, eight, nine, and ten can all be produced by multiplying previous numbers in the series together. And the other prime numbers within the series of the first ten (two, three, five) can all be multiplied by one of the proceeding numbers to produce a result which is contained in the series of the first ten.

It is interesting to note at this point that the Tetragrammaton, or Hebrew name of God, bears a strong visual resemblance to the number 777, as can be readily seen below:

Indeed, the number 777 has often been used as a way of depicting the name of God or the Tetragrammaton (obviously in contrast with the number of the beast, 666). While it is tempting to dismiss this visual resemblance as mere coincidence, the graphic forms of our Arabic numbers (as used in the number 777) are all originally of Semitic origin.

The significance and uniqueness of seven also lies in the fact that it is the result of the addition of three and four. In this respect, we have represented mystically the union of the Divinity (through the Holy Trinity, obviously represented by three), and human nature—represents by four, which correspond with the four actions of virtue of the human soul.

Translator's note

The four 'actions of virtue' referred to here are the same as the traditional four 'cardinal virtues' (prudence, justice, fortitude, and temperance), which are discussed in the earlier chapter on the number four. Readers should note that these four cardinal virtues, in addition to the three theological virtues (faith, hope, and charity), likewise make a total of seven. Sometimes, (erroneously) it is assumed that these seven virtues (the four cardinal virtues, plus the three theological virtues) are the 'seven cardinal virtues,' mirroring the 'seven cardinal vices' (or 'seven deadly sins'). Some (but not all) of the 'seven gifts of the Holy Spirit' (wisdom, understanding, counsel, fortitude, knowledge, piety, and fear of the Lord) coincide with these virtues.

This conjunction of the mystery of Trinity together with the four cardinal virtues of the human soul in the number seven is of the highest importance in appreciating its mystical meaning. For it is only through the grace of the Trinity and the contemplation of this mystery that the four cardinal virtues can be brought to their perfection. Yet it is also only through the cultivation of these four cardinal virtues that the soul becomes capable of knowledge of, and entrance into the mystery of, the Holy Trinity.

The mystical connection between three and four (the Trinity of the Godhead and the four cardinal virtues of the human soul) is represented not only in seven (formed by adding them together), but also in the number of twelve (arrived at by multiplying three and four). The mystical meaning of twelve shall be discussed later, but it was through the four cardinal virtues in the twelve apostles that faith in the Trinity was spread throughout the world. Again, the mystical connection or union between three and four (Divinity and humanity) is manifested in the fact that the twelve (3 x 4) apostles received the seven (3 + 4) gifts of the Holy Spirit.

The number seven represents also the complete duration of this universe. For, although it was in six days that the world was created, the seventh day (the day of rest) is added to represent its consummation. And similarly, while there are six ages in the history of humanity,[65] the addition of one more reflects the consummation or end of this series of ages. And finally (as described in the previous chapter), there are six stages in the life of man (infancy, childhood, adolescence, young adulthood, maturity, and finally old age). The addition of one more, death, brings a total of seven, and thus represents not only the entire duration of human life, but also its consummation or completion. Thus, the number seven expresses perfectly not only all the stages but also the completion or consummation of the universe, the history of humanity, and the life of the individual human being. And this consummation or fulfillment, represented mystically through seven, is achieved only through the union of Divinity (signified by three) and humanity (signified by four).

---

[65] See Chapter Six.

And while the number signifies both the bringing to completion or consummation of history and the ultimate purpose of the universe and life itself, it also more particularly represents rest. For it was on the seventh day that God ceased from His work of creation and rested, and commanded human beings to do likewise on the Sabbath. In connection with this symbolism of peace, seven mystically indicates also the unity of the Church of God. This unity is throughout all the world, and also throughout all time. Hence we find written in the psalm: "Seven times a day shall I praise Thee."[66] In other words, the entire Church shall praise God for all eternity, and this act of praise represents full consummation, or the enjoyment of the ultimate rest and the perpetual peace of the everlasting Sabbath of Heaven. The fact that the praise represented by the expression "seven times" is actually eternal is made manifested when the Psalmist, expressing the same reality, says that "His praise [will be] *always* on my lips."[67]

The fact that seven signifies the eternal rest of Heaven is reflected and embodied in His commandment for the seventh day of each week to be sanctified and held as a day of rest.[68] The traditional Hebrew Sabbath, as specified in Scripture, commences on the evening of the sixth day,

---

66 Psalm 118:164.
67 Psalm 33:1.
68 See Hebrews 4:1–8.

and then concludes before the evening of the seventh day itself[69]—meaning that the Sabbath itself does not conclude with evening, and there is thus no twilight to conclude or terminate this day of rest. This mystically symbolizes the eternal nature of the beatitude of Heaven, the day without end on which the sun of glory and happiness never sets.[70]

The fact that seven likewise signifies the entire Church is found in the fact that when He appeared to some of the disciples after the Resurrection on the shores of the Sea of Galilee and prepared a breakfast of fish for them, it was specifically to seven of the disciples who were present.[71] Similarly, when the apostle John addressed his letters to the various churches of the world at the beginning of his Apocalypse, it is to seven particular churches that he writes.[72] By this is signified the entirety of the Church, both in place and time, enriched and identified as it is by the sevenfold gifts of the Holy Spirit. This unity of the perfect Church, or the Church in its consummation, is expressed beautifully in the Song of Songs, in which the Lord speaks of His mystical Spouse (i.e., the Church), saying of Her lovingly: "One is my dove, one is my perfect one!"[73] And so the

---

69 See Nahum 13:19; Leviticus 23:32.

70 See Hebrews 3:13.

71 See John 21:1–10. The seven who were present were the apostles Peter, Thomas, Nathaniel, James, John, and two unnamed disciples. See John 21:2.

72 See Revelation 1:11.

73 Cant. 6:8.

number seven, paradoxically, represents the same mystical and sacred unity as one itself does. This same holy unity, expressed in both seven and one, reflects the unity of the Deity, the unity of the Church, and the union of divine nature and human virtue (symbolized by three and four respectively) through the mystery of the Incarnation of Our Lord Jesus Christ.

Translator's note

This mystical convergence of seven and one (in that they both symbolize a mystical unity or union) is presented here wonderfully and with great clarity and inspiration by Saint Isidore. It is interesting to note that the three and four which together form the sacred number of seven, and represent God and the human being respectively, are separated only by one. But this one, though the difference or separation between the two components (the numbers three and four), is also, by its very nature, itself a unity or union. Thus, what is termed the 'hypostatic union' of Divine and human natures (symbolized by three and four) in Christ is mystically signified in both the seven (the results of the union) and the one (the union itself, as well as the connection/difference between the two elements [three and four] which produce the union). And readers will recall from the chapter on the number one or unity that this one itself symbolically betokens the Supreme Unity, which is God, as well as the unity of the human being, reflecting the image of God.

Though Isidore does not mention in this treatise the connection of the number six with Lucifer (found most conspicuously in the number of the beast, 666, in Revelation 13:8), the present translator suggests an important way in which six contrasts with seven. For six is the result of two threes being added together, or being juxtaposed. Since three represents symbolically the mystery of the Triune God, do the two threes which form six exhibit the sin of Lucifer's pride, who claimed for himself, or attempted to attain, equality in status with God? But in the case of seven (three and four joined together) the union is not one of pretended equality, but rather acknowledges the inequality between the two elements. Yet, paradoxically, the inequality between three and four is one, which is itself an expression of union, and itself divine.

It is indeed fitting that the gifts of the Holy Spirit should be seven in number. This Spirit rested on or dwelt within Christ, as the prophet Isaiah testifies: "And the Spirit of the Lord rested upon Him—a Spirit of wisdom and understanding, a Spirit of counsel and fortitude, a Spirit of knowledge and piety, and this Spirit filled Him with fear of the Lord."[74] The graces of gifts of this Holy Spirit are thus sevenfold. Now seven, as has been noted, represents consummation or bringing to fulfillment, as in the seven days of creation (when the consummation or rest day is

[74] Isaias 11:2. See also John 1:32–33, in which the Holy Spirit, in the form of a dover, is described as resting upon Christ.

included), and in the many other examples provided. This reflects that Christ Himself, upon whom the Spirit with its sevenfold graces, rested, is Himself the consummation or fulfilment of the eternal plan or destiny of creation and salvation, of both humanity and of all the cosmos.

It is in accordance with this reality that the prophet Zechariah witnessed in a vision a stone with seven eyes, laid before the high priest, Joshua.[75] Now this seven-eyed stone represents none other than Christ Himself, who is described elsewhere in Scripture as being a rock.[76]

Other examples of the sacred number of seven are to be found in a marvelous abundance in the pages of Sacred Scripture. There were seven generations from Adam and Enoch.[77] Lamech is also in the seventh generation from Adam.[78] To anyone who would murder Cain, a sevenfold vengeance was threatened.[79] And to anyone who would slay Lamech, a seventy-seven-fold vengeance was reserved.[80]

Translator's note

Although Lamech (the father of Noah) is a grandson of Enoch in Genesis 5, he like Enoch, are both identified as being the seventh generation from Adam. This is because Enoch is in the

---

75 See Josue 3:9.
76 See 1 Corinthians 10:4.
77 See Genesis 5.
78 See Genesis 5.
79 Genesis 4:24.
80 Genesis 4:24.

seventh generation through the line of Seth (Adam's third son, after Cain and Abel),[81] *but Lamech's ancestry can be traced either through Seth or through Cain (both being sons of Adam). Following the line of Cain's descendants, in Genesis 5, Lamech is in the seventh generation from Adam (although he is the ninth generation, following the line of descent of Seth). Interestingly, Lamech, who was protected by the threat of a seventy-seven-fold vengeance on anyone who killed him, lived for 777 years. See Genesis 5:31.*

Although Saint Isidore does not mention it at this point, Christ's direction to forgive "not seven times but seventy-seven times"[82] *can be understood in relation to the demand for sevenfold and seventy-seven-fold vengeance for Cain and Lamech respectively. Here, forgiveness effectively replaces vengeance, in accordance with Our Lord's own teaching.*

It was on the seventh day after Noah had entered the ark that the rains of the great deluge began to fall.[83] Then it was in the seventh month of the flood that the ark finally came to rest on solid ground.[84] And Noah had been instructed to bring seven pairs of each species of clean animal into the ark.[85]

---

81 See Genesis 4:25.

82 Matthew 18:22.

83 See Genesis 7:10.

84 See Genesis 8:10. Interestingly, it is specified that the ark came to rests on the 17th day of the seventh month.

85 See Genesis 7:2–3.

It was commanded that the Passover should be celebrated for a period of seven days each year.[86] And also Moses, the law-giver, set up a seven-branched golden candelabrum over the Ark of the Covenant.[87]

There are to be found a great many more examples in which the sacred number of seven symbolizes the consummation of God's plan, and the mystical union of divinity and humanity. We list just a few of the more prominent cases below:

- When the Ark of the Covenant was taken around the city of Jericho, causing its walls to come tumbling down, it was surrounded by seven trumpets. It is taken around the city seven times, for seven days.[88]
- When the prophet Elisha raised a dead boy to life, he prayed seven times.[89]
- The prophet Isaiah speaks of a time to come in which seven women will attempt to lay hands on each man.[90]

---

[86] See Exodus 12:15–20.

[87] See Exodus 25:31–40. This candelabrum, known as a menorah in the Hebrew tradition, is described as having three branches on either side, as well as one central branch, giving a total of seven. See Exodus 25:37.

[88] See Josue 6.

[89] See 1 Kings 18:43–46.

[90] See Is. 4:1.

- When the Sadducees attempt to trap Christ concerning the resurrection of the dead, they propose to Him a situation in which a certain woman has been married to some seven different brothers in succession.[91]
- In the Gospel, it is related the Christ feed a multitude with seven loaves of bread, and that seven baskets of leftovers were collected afterwards.[92]
- The apostle Saint Paul wrote letters to seven different churches—namely the churches of the Romans, the Corinthians, the Galatians, the Ephesians, the Philippians, the Colossians, and the Thessalonians.
- Saint John, in the Apocalypse, saw Christ surrounded by seven golden candelabra, which represent the seven churches to which he writes—namely the churches of Ephesus, to Smyrna, to Pergamum, to Thyatira, to Sardis, to Philadelphia, and to Laodicea.[93]
- In the same Apocalypse of Saint John, it is written that there are seven stars in the right hand of God;[94] it is the seventh seal on a book which the Lamb that has been slain is alone

[91] See Matthew 22:23–34; Mark 12:18–27; Luke 20:27–40.
[92] Matthew 15:32–39; Mark 8:1–9.
[93] See Revelation 1:4, 1:11.
[94] Revelation 1:16.

> able to open;[95] seven angels sound on seven trumpets; and there are seven plagues which afflict the earth.[96]

This number, seven, when multiplied by itself, and then the mystery of the unity added, produces the 50 (i.e., [7 x 7] + 1 = 50). Now it was on the 50th day that the Holy Spirit, with its sevenfold gifts, descended upon the apostles at Pentecost. Similarly, the same number of 50, formed by the multiplication of the sacred seven and the addition of the mystery of the divine Unity, marks the year of Jubilee, which is kept perpetually as a time of peace, liberation, forgiveness, and the remission of debts.[97]

There is also sometimes the case that this sacred number of seven is used in relation to things which evil. For example, we encounter in the Apocalypse a beast having seven heads,[98] and the seven cardinal vices (or deadly sins) are seven in number—namely pride, envy, anger, sloth, greed, gluttony, and lust. In such cases, it is not that seven is itself evil, but rather it is used to indicate a contrariness or opposition to the sacred. Thus, the seven-headed beast is assigned seven heads because it exists in opposition to the

---

95 See Revelation 8.

96 See Revelation 8–11.

97 See Leviticus 8:25–38. "Count off seven Sabbath years—seven times seven years—so that the seven Sabbath years amount to a period of forty-nine years." Leviticus 8:25.

98 See Revelation 13.

Holy Spirit with its seven graces. And the seven cardinal vices represent opposition to the total of seven virtues (that is, the three theological virtues and the four cardinal virtues, or virtues of the human soul).[99]

So it is that the number of instances in which the number seven is of mystical significance in Sacred Scripture are virtually infinite. But we shall now pass to some important cases outside the realms of Scripture, for these are also deeply significant and reflect the same profound symbolic meaning permeating the entire cosmos. Among the ancients, it was always held that there were seven branches of philosophy—the first being arithmetic; the second, geometry; the third, music; the fourth, astronomy; the fifth, astrology; the sixth, mechanics; and the seventh, medicine. Again, the forms or stages of the moon are seven—the first being *bicornis* ('two-horned'); the second is the *sectilis* ('able to be cut into layers'), which is also called the *mediluna* ('medium moon'); the third is the *dimidia* ('half'); the fourth and central phase in the *plena* ('full'); the fifth phase is once again the *dimidia*; the sixth phase is again the *sectilis*; and the seventh and final stage is the same as the first, the *bicornis*.[100] The three final stages here repeat the

---

[99] See Chapter Four.

[100] The identification and arrangement of the phases of the moon given here by Saint Isidore reflect those used in the classical and Medieval world. Modern astronomy uses eight phases, or, rather, nine, if one counts them as did Saint Isidore, so that the final stage (which is identical with the first) is counted at both the beginning and the end—giving the new moon, waxing crescent, first quarter, waxing gibbous, full

first three stages in reversed order, around the central stage, which is, of course, the full moon.[101]

The fact that the stages of the moon are seven is highly significant. For if the first seven numbers (1, 2, 3, 4, 5, 6, and 7) are all added together, the result is 28, which is the full number days in a complete cycle of the moon.

Again, there are seven circles of the Heavens, each of which is ruled by one of the seven planets—namely, the Moon, Mercury, Venus, the Sun, Mars, Jupiter, and Saturn.

Translator's note

*This conception of the Heavens as consisting of seven spheres in classical cosmography is similarly found in many other cultures and traditions. In the Hebrew tradition, there are seven Heavens—*Vilon *(וילון, see Isaiah 40:22),* Raki'a *(רקיע, see Genesis 1:17),* Shehaqim *(שחקים, Ps 78:23),* Zebul *(זבול, see Isaiah 63:15 and 1 Kings 8:13),* Ma'on *(מעון, see Deuteronomy 26:1),* Machon *(מכון, see 1 Kings 8:39 and Deuteronomy 28:12), and* Araboth *(ערבות). Similarly, in Islam, it is believed that there are seven Heavens. And in the Puranas,*

---

moon, waning gibbous, third quarter, and waning crescent, and finally the new moon once again. This difference in numbering is created by the modern scheme using an additional division of the partially visible moon.

[101] Readers will note that this symmetrical scheme of seven phases of the moon (with three symmetrical or mirrored parts on either side of a central part, which is the greatest or highest) corresponds to the arrangement of the branches of the seven-branched golden candelabrum, or menorah, placed on the Ark of the Covenant. See Exodus 25:37.

or holy epics of Hinduism, there are likewise said to be seven upper worlds, as well as seven lower worlds.

Similarly, there are seven days of the week, and there are seven transfusions or transformations of the elements. For out of fire is born air; out of air is born water; out of water is born earth; and out of the earth is born water; out of water is born air; and finally, out of air is born fire.

The human body is composed of seven sections or levels—namely the head and neck, the chest, the abdomen, the pelvis, the thigh, the shank, and the foot. And it is said by physicians that it is on the seventh day of any illness that the life of a patient is most greatly imperiled. And in the Greek alphabet, seven vowels are to be found—alpha (α,) epsilon (ε), eta (η), iota (ι), omicron (ο), upsilon (υ), and omega (ω).

Within the head of a human being there are seven receptacles for the reception of sensory data—the two eyes, the two ears, the two nostrils, and the one mouth. In infants, it is seven months before the teeth begin to emerge, and in the seventh year of human life that the infant teeth fall out, to be replaced by the adult teeth. It is after the second set of seven years that young people begin to become mature, that is, that they are able to procreate. It is in the third set of seven years (i.e., between the ages of 21 and 28) that the beard of men and the glow of women's cheeks flourishes most strongly. It is at the commencement of fourth set of seven years of human life (i.e., at 28 years of age) that greatest height or stature and strength of body is attained. At the beginning of the fifth set of seven years (i.e., at the age of 35), the period of youthfulness and development has reached it end. In the sixth set of seven years of human life (i.e., from the ages of 42 to 49), vigor and strength enter into the stage of decline. And finally, at the beginning of the seventh set of seven years of life (at 50 years of age), the period of a person being old has commenced.

Again, there are seven principal organs which serve the digestive and circulatory processes of the human body—the tongue, the heart, the lungs, the liver, the spleen, and two kidneys. And the human body is formed from seven members of limbs—the head, neck, chest, abdomen, together with two arms and the two legs. This arrangement of the human body shows that it is indeed a microcosm (or miniature universe), corresponding in form, and intended to be in harmony with, the macrocosm, or great universe. For the macrocosm, or great universe (as has been noted), itself comprises seven celestial spheres or Heavens.

EIGHT

THE NUMBER EIGHT belongs to that special series of numbers formed by doubling the preceding one (1, 2, 4, 8, 16 . . .). It is a holy number, and this is represented in the fact that, according to the Old Law, circumcision occurs on the eighth day.[102] This earthly circumcision was a figure or symbol of the 'true circumcision,' or the entrance into new and eternal life. It is the first number to follow the sacred number of seven, and may be said to emerge out of that sacred number. If the creation of the universe took place in seven days (including the final day of rest), the newly formed universe may be said to have commenced its functioning or life on the eighth day of its existence. Hence it is fitting that the eighth day of the week coincides with the first day of the new week, representing the commencement of a new period of time or age.

[102] See Leviticus 12:3; Luke 2:21.

As noted in the previous chapter, the number seven represents the consummation of fulfilment of life. Thus it is that the number eight mystically symbolizes the commencement of the new and eternal life, which follows the consummation of the present one. Fittingly, therefore, it was on the eighth day of the week, which is a Sunday (and which coincides with the first day of the week which follow), that Our Lord rose from the dead. The number eight therefore is a sign of the hope of eternal beatitude promised in and through the Resurrection.

It is fitting therefore that we find the following otherwise mysterious injunction in Sacred Scripture: "Give a portion to seven, and also to eight; for you do not know what evils lie ahead on earth."[103] This is conveying the same message, in symbolically expressed form, as the following wise and holy counsel: "Deal with passing matters carefully, and in such a way that you always consider them in relation to those things which are eternal. For you do not know what the future judgment will bring to you."

Translator's note

This counsel is not referenced by Isidore, but seems to be a paraphrase of a oft-quoted piece of advice found in Saint Gregory the Great's Moralia on Job, which reads: "Deal with passing matters in such a way that you do not cease to long for that

[103] Ecclus. 11:2.

which is eternal." Saint Isidore and Saint Gregory the Great knew each other well, and they read and profoundly esteemed and respected each other's writings. It was Gregory who appointed Isidore as Vicar Apostolic of all Spain.

The number eight also represents the union of the Lord, who is One, with His Body, the Church, which (as noted in the previous chapter) is mystically symbolized by seven. Accordingly, Noah entered the ark accompanied by seven other people, giving a total of eight human beings.[104] Seven of these, apart from Noah, represent the entire Church in its unity; while the eighth, Noah himself, is a figure of Christ, who is the Head of the Church.

The same symbolic meaning is conveyed in the book of the prophet Micah, in which he speaks of "seven shepherds and eight principal men."[105] The seven shepherds represent the Church and its pastors, but the eighth (who, together with these seven shepherds, form the eight principal men referred to) is Christ Himself, the chief Shepherd.

The number eight is encountered at several vital points in the Gospel also, where it presents the same mystical significance of the commencement of a new era or life. Thus we are specifically told, for example, that it was eight days after Christ had predicted that some of those present would not taste death before they saw the Kingdom of God that

---

[104] See Genesis 7:13.

[105] See Micah 5:5.

He revealed His glorious nature in the Transfiguration.[106] This event is strongly connected with the meaning of the commencement of a new era or age, for His manifestation in radiance at the Transfiguration was a revelation of the future new life of eternal blessedness, and an expression of the fact that, in Him, it had already begun.

Again, the Savior appeared to Thomas (known as the Twin), who had initially refused to believe, eight days after His Resurrection—again manifesting the newness of the Resurrected life.[107]

When eight is multiplied by the three, which signifies the mystery of the Trinity, the result is twenty-four. This is reflected in the fact that, in the vision recorded in the Apocalypse, it is twenty-four elders who cast down their crowns in the presence of the Lamb as a sign of their worship of the One who represents the commencement of the new and eternal age of glory and beatitude.[108]

---

[106] See Luke 9:27–36.

[107] See John 20:24–29. Note that in John 20, it is recounted that Christ appeared to Mary Magdalene on the morning of the Resurrection, and to the other apostles (except for Thomas) on the evening of the same day. See John 20:19. It is then specified that one week later (i.e., on the eighth day after the Resurrection) that He appeared in the presence of Thomas. See John 20:26. As an aside, reader may note the fact that Thomas is described as "the Twin" brings in the number two, which, as noted in the chapter on the mystical meaning of that number, carries within it the possibility of disagreement or conflict. The fact that Thomas poses, at least initially, the view of unbelief in opposition to the belief of the other apostles, is a notable example of this symbolism.

[108] See Revelation 4:10–11.

The number eight sometimes appears also in relation to an evil or sinister aspect. For example, in the vision of Saint John, it is the eighth of the kings of Rome who is the beast and a figure of the devil.[109] And there are the eight principal vices—namely envy, wrath, sadness, avarice, gluttony, lust, vain glory, and pride. It is out of these vices that all the others emerge. In these cases, the number eight similarly symbolizes the possibility of the commencement of a new era or state; but it is not here one of blessedness and eternal life, but rather one of wretchedness and evil.

Translator's note

The text pertaining to this eighth king in the Apocalypse reads thus: "The seven heads are seven hills, upon which the woman sits, and they are seven kings. Five of these have fallen, one still is, and the other has not yet come: and when he has come, he must remain only a short time. And the beast which was, and is not: the same beast is also the eighth king. He is of the seven, and he leads to destruction." Revelation 17:9–11.

The eight vices mentioned here refer to the 'eight thoughts' or logismoi *identified by Evagrius of Pontus, which are given by him as gluttony, lust, avarice, sadness, wrath, acedia (boredom), vainglory, and pride. This list eventually gave rise to the concepts of the 'seven capital vices,' with the closely related viced of sadness (meaning here a kind of emotional lethargy) and acedia (meaning a kind of boredom or laziness) being merged into the single vice of sloth, which encompasses them both.*

[109] See Revelation 17:9–11.

NINE

NINE IS, ACCORDING to itself, a perfect number. In a way, it is of particular perfection or completeness, since it is the product of multiplying three—a number which represents perfection since, as noted in the chapter on that number, it contains a beginning, middle, and end within itself.

But, viewed in another way, nine also mystically portrays imperfection. For it closely approaches the end of the series of the first ten numbers, and yet it always falls just short of this end. It is close to it, and would reach the goal of goal of ten if one more unit were added—but it does not. In this sense, it represents those who attempt to or strive to follow the precepts of God (in other words, people who know what these commandments are and know that they should be followed), and yet somehow fail to do so.[110]

[110] See James 2:10. "And whosoever shall keep the whole law, but offend in one point, becomes guilty of all."

The number of nine therefore fittingly appears in the Gospel in relation to the incident of the nine lepers who approach Christ and are healed by Him, [but then fail to give thanks. For out of the ten who originally approach Him,] it is only one who gives thanks to his Divine Healer.[111] Of these nine, it is only one who gives thanks to his divine Healer. As for the other nine, because of the fact that they are in an apparently numerous consort, none of them give due thanks, out of negligence, ingratitude, and a certain pride or presumption because of the fact that they are a sizeable group.

Another example which exhibits this same mystical sense of the imperfection of nine is in the parable of the hundred sheep.[112] It is only one of these sheep which becomes lost, and which the Shepherd restores by carrying it upon His shoulders; while ninety-nine of them are not lost at all. This parable represents not the fact that only one person out of many goes astray and requires rescuing by the Shepherd, but rather that only one person of the many *recognizes* their own need for penance and redemption. The other ninety-nine fail to acknowledge and understand their need for penance. Seeing so many others who are apparently doing exactly the same as themselves, they assume that they are not lost or in need of being saved at all.

[111] See Luke 17:11–19.
[112] See Matthew 18:12–14; Luke 15:3–7.

Translator's note

The parable of the women with the ten drachmas, who loses one, may readily also be added as another case of this same symbolic meaning of the number nine.[113]

But to return to the first symbolism of nine, as the sign of completion resulting from multiplying three with itself, the Hebrews acknowledge nine books of the prophets. And the ancient Greeks and Romans believed that there were nine Muses, which together represent the completion or perfection of the arts.

Translator's note

Saint Isidore's reference to the Hebrews acknowledging nine books of the prophets has not been able to be identified with certainty by the present translator, and the traditions in circulation at his time in Spain may not necessarily match contemporary Jewish classifications of the Scriptures. Since the twelve minor Prophets are counted as a single book in the Hebrew tradition, together with the books of the four 'former prophets' (Joshua, Judges, Samuel, and Kings), the three 'latter prophets' (Isaiah, Jeremiah, and Ezekiel), and the writings attributed to Moses (the Pentateuch, counting this as the writings of one prophet), there are then 'nine books of the prophets.' But this suggestion is advanced only as a conjecture.

113 See Luke 15:8–10.

The nine Muses of the classical world were Calliope (responsible for the discipline of epic poetry), Clio (responsible for history), Polyhymnia (responsible for hymnody), Euterpe (responsible for performance on the flute), Terpsichore (responsible for dancing), Erato (responsible for light and choral poetry), Melpomene (responsible for tragedy), Thalia (responsible for comedy), and Urania (responsible for astronomy and astrology). Together, they were understood as representing the liberal and creative arts in completion.

TEN

THE NUMBER TEN is to be deeply respected and esteemed, as it contains within itself the virtues of every other number. It is also the completion of the series of the first decade. It completes the unity of the first decade, and this first decade is itself an image or magnified form of the unity. It represents also the opening up of the first series of numbers or the first complete decade or set onto everything which follows—in fact, an opening out of the virtues and potentialities of the complete set of basic numbers into a multitude, and even to the extent of infinity.

In Sacred Scripture, ten is used to represent the will of God and His righteousness. It sometimes signifies perfection, but also the arrival at completion or totality. An example of this is to be found in the book of the prophet Daniel. When he wishes to represent the totality of the Church, or perhaps the totality of host of the holy angels, he says "a thousand times a thousand will minister to Him."[114] Now, this thousand is here an amplification or magnification of the meaning and symbolism of ten (being ten multiplied by itself, then multiplied by itself once more). And in the psalms, similar symbolism is employed, such as when we read: "The chariots of God are thousands upon thousands of those rejoicing."[115]

Very significantly, ten is the number of the principal commandments of God, which are, for this reason, known as the Decalogue or 'Ten Words.' In this respect, they are to be understood as representing the complete or totality of the will of God.

From Adam until Noah, there were ten generations.[116] And the prophet David performed upon a lyre of ten-strings, known as a decachord.[117] And King Solomon, his son, placed ten candelabra in the Temple of God, five to the left and five to the right of the altar.[118] The choice of ten candelabra was to form an image or likeness of the ten-stringed lyre or harp of his father David, which represents the whole of psalmody and sacred song with which the Lord is praised and glorified, or the entire act of worship of God.

---

[114] Dan. 7:10.
[115] Psalm 72:18.
[116] See 1 Chronicles 1:1–4. The generations were Adam, Seth, Enosh, Kenan, Mahalalel, Jared, Enoch, Methuselah, Lamech, and Noah.
[117] See Psalm 32:2, 91:4, and 143:9.
[118] See Chronicles 4:7.

In the book of the prophet Zachariah, we hear of a vision of some ten men, who strive to take hold of a Judean by his coat.[119] These ten men represent the totality of the Church, who are those who cling to the hem of the cloak of the Christ and finding healing and salvation therefrom.

In the Gospel, there is the parable of the ten virgins.[120] These ten virgins, five of whom are described as wise while the other five are foolish, together represent the five senses, applied in a twofold way—that is, to both the body and the soul. When the data of the five senses is judged only according to the impulses of the body, the result is the five foolish virgins. But when this five-fold sensory data is used properly and prudently, and ruled by the higher faculty of the mind, this is represented by the five wise virgins. Hence the ten virgins, five of whom are wise and five of whom are foolish, represent the potential for both foolish and prudent use of the human senses. For the same senses which lead us to understanding and wisdom can also draw us into sin and error.

There were, as noted in the previous chapter, some ten lepers who were healed by Christ as a group.[121] Now only one of these lepers remained to thank the Lord. The other nine separated from this one—in this way, they represent

---

119 See Zacharias 23:8.
120 See Matthew 25.
121 See Luke 17:11–19.

those who separate themselves from unity, both the unity of the Church, and the Supreme Unity of God.

Next, we are told of the servant assigned custody of ten talents by his Master, who, because he managed these wisely and profitably, was promised rulership of ten cities in the future. These ten talents are, like the ten virgins, a representation of the five senses of the body, applied both to the body and to the soul (and therefore multiplied by two). The parable signifies that if all of these senses are governed wisely and well-controlled, both in respect to acts of the body and to acts of the mind or heart, a Heavenly reward shall certainly be attained, in the form of the life to come. And just as an entire city is of vastly greater value than a single talent, so will the future reward be incomparably superior to anything in this life.

Ten is used also to signify suffering, trials, or the administering of fitting punishment. In these cases, the number ten signifies that such things, while dreadful in themselves, happen in accordance with the will and justice of God; and so the symbolism of the number ten as representing divine law and justice is very apt for such cases. For example, in the book of Exodus there are some ten plagues which strike the Egyptians.[122] In the Apocalypse, a ten-horned,

---

[122] See Exodus 7–11.

seven-headed beast proceeds out of the sea,[123] and ten days of suffering or trial for the Church spoken of.[124]

But these examples of the symbolism of the number ten shall suffice.

We have now spoken of all the numbers of the primary series, or the first decade. This first decade of numbers presents within itself the rules and principles for the interpretation of the mystical meaning of all numbers, which can be extrapolated or deduced from them. Each of the first ten numbers is deeply symbolic in itself; and these numbers do not appear in Sacred Scripture without conveying something which is spiritually significant to the reader who is equipped with the knowledge and insight to penetrate their hidden and mystical meanings.

We may summarize these meanings below:

- *One* is not a number itself, but is the origin of all things, symbolizing the primal Unity which is of God Himself.
- *Two* signifies an equality or comparability, and the emergence of connection or relationship;

123 See Revelation 13:1.
124 See Revelation 2:10.

this connection or relationship is what makes possible all action and interaction, as well as both harmony and conflict.

- *Three* may be understood as being first in virtue, for it is the first number to contain within itself perfection or the elements of completion—that is, it has a beginning, a middle, and an end. Thus it represents the mystery of the nature of God, which, although supremely One, is also a Trinity.
- *Four* consists of two equal twos, and represents solidity or strength, or firmness of foundation.
- *Five* is a unique number, representing the law of God.
- *Six* represents the totality or entirety of works, actions, and ages, in both the universe, in man, and in particular human acts.
- *Seven* is a sacred number. Whereas six represent simply a *totality* of components or elements, seven represent a *consummation* or *fulfillment.*
- *Eight* is part of the series of numbers formed by successive doublings (1, 2, 4, 8, 16, etc.), and represents the emergence of newness from something which has been brought to its consummation.

- *Nine* is perfect in one sense, as three multiplied by itself. Yet it is also used to express imperfection, or a falling short of some goal or purpose (symbolized by ten).
- *Ten* is the completion of the first decade. It contains within itself the symbolism of unity, and is a magnification or amplification of the number one. It is related also to the symbolism of five, which was principally that of the law of God. Ten represents the *will* of God, or the *justice* of God.

We shall consider also two numbers beyond the limits of the first decade in the chapters that follow.

ELEVEN

ELEVEN IS THE first number in the second decade or group of ten. In the Sacred Scriptures, the number eleven is generally used to indicate sin, or the transgression of the precepts or laws of God, since ten (as noted in the previous chapter) represents the law or justice of God. Hence it is that the eleventh psalm begins thus: "Save me, O Lord, for piety is failing, and truth is vanishing from among the children of men."[125] Just as ten indicates the perfection of obedience to God and the happiness which springs from perfect conformity to His will, so eleven indicates a breaking away from this obedience and departure from, or transgression of, the will of God.

Accordingly, we find that it was in the eleventh generation of human beings from Adam (counting through the line of Cain) that the great flood occurred. Now this flood

[125] Psalm 11:2.

was sent as a direct result of the flourishing of sin and transgression among humanity.

Translator's note

Readers may recall that in the previous chapter, Isidore mentioned that there were ten generations between Adam to Noah. But this number is following the line of Seth (signifying God's justice). This alternative numbering, signifying transgression or sin, is, appropriately, through Cain. The generations of mankind through Cain are listed in Genesis 6 as being Adam, Cain, Enoch, Irad, Mehujael, Methuselah, Lamech, then Noah (among the children of Lamech). But, as Isidore points out in his commentary on Genesis 6 (in his Quaestiones in Veterum Testamentum*), there were, in fact, three sons and one daughter born to Lamech, which should be added to this numbering of generations. In that commentary, he writes:*

> *Truly the fact that the progeny of Adam through Cain came to its end after eleven generations represents transgression of the commandments of God (symbolized by ten), or sin, and reveals that transgression shall be brought to an end by God's justice. For while we read that Lamech (the father of Noah) was the seventh generation from Adam (through the line of Cain), there must be added to this number of generations of Lamech's own offspring which were born before Noah, who (in addition to Noah) were three sons and one*

daughter.[126] *Through this number, eleven, sin or transgression is signified, which was the cause of the flood.*

In the book of Exodus, it is specified that there should be eleven veils of sackcloth, or coarse goats' hair, made to cover the top of the tabernacle. Since the number eleven signifies sin or transgression of the law, it is fitting that these veils of sackcloth which cover the top of the tabernacle of the Temple should also be eleven in number, representing penitence for each of the sins signified by eleven.[127]

In the book of the prophet Daniel also a beast with eleven horns is described.[128] This represents the fact that it is the devil himself who is the author of transgression. It symbolizes also the son of the devil, the Antichrist, and how his kingdom will flourish for a time when the power of sin is exalted.

The symbolism of sin and transgression by the number eleven is important among the apostles. For after Judas had proved to be a traitor and had taken his own life, Peter promptly appointed a replacement for him, in the person of Matthias, who was chosen by lot.[129] He did this lest the number of apostles should remain at eleven, the number symbolizing transgression. In this instance, indeed, the

---

[126] See Genesis 4:20–22.

[127] See Exodus 27:8.

[128] See Daniel 7:7–8. This beast initially has ten horns (Daniel 7:7) but then another, eleventh horn springs up and begins to speak blasphemies (Daniel 7:8).

[129] See Acts of the Apostles 1:20–26.

number of eleven had particular force and unmistakable clarity in this symbolism, since the number of eleven apostles (which was quickly restored to twelve) was the direct and visible consequence of the sin of the treachery of Judas, and his transgression beyond faith in Christ.

The number eleven figures with significance also in times and dates, and in that context does not have any evil significance. For example, the world is believed to have been created on the eleventh day before the Calends of April.

Translator's Note

This eleventh day before the Calends (or first day) of April is March 22. Traditionally, this was held to be the date of the creation of the earth, with Adam and Eve being created on March 25. March 25 was also the date of the Annunciation to the Blessed Virgin Mary, and is believed to have been the original calendar date of the crucifixion of the Lord. It was on this same calendar date (March 25) that the following events have also traditionally been believed to have occurred:

- *The victory of the archangel Saint Michael over the devil;*
- *The murder of Abel by his brother Cain;*
- *The crossing of the Red Sea by the Israelites;*
- *The appearance of the high priest Melchizedek; and,*
- *Abraham's offering of his son Isaac in obedience to the Lord.*

The belief that the world was created on a date connected with, or counted from, the Calends of April (April 1) led to celebration of the commencement of the New Year on this date in many parts of Europe. The custom of celebrating the New Year on April 1 persisted in parts of rural France until relatively recent times, and this is what gave rise to the popular identification of this day with April Fools' Day.

TWELVE

THE NUMBER TWELVE is among the other important numbers which are held to be especially sacred. It is closely related to the number seven, for twelve is the product of the multiplication of the components of that number (i.e., three, which signifies the mystery of the divinity, and four, which signifies humanity and the virtues of the human soul). When either four is multiplied by three, or three is multiplied by four, the result is twelve; just as when three is added to four, or four added to three, the number seven is produced.

There is also another unique property of twelve which makes it of particular mystical significance. For it has a remarkable property of harmonious divisibility. This number can be divided into twelve equal parts, each part being one; and it can be divided into six equal parts, each part being two; or, again, into three equal parts, each part being four; or into four equal parts, each part being three; or into six equal parts, each part being two; and finally into twelve equal parts, each part being one. Thus, it can be divided in six possible ways, each of which yields an equal and complete result. This number of possible harmonious divisions, relative to its total magnitude, is not exceeded by that of any other number.

Translator's note

A little consideration that this observation offered by Isidore is quite correct. Twelve can be divided evenly into six possible fractional divisions, which is equal to half its total magnitude. The other numbers which have a relatively high possible number of divisions do not equal this. For example, eight can be divided equally into eighths, quarters, and halves—a total of three possible equal divisions, which is less than half its magnitude. Twenty-four can be divided into twenty-fourths, twelfths, eighths, sixths, quarters, thirds, and halves—a total of seven possible even divisions, which is less than half its magnitude. The single exception is six, which can be divided into three possible even divisions—sixths, halves, and thirds. In this case, it does equal, but does not exceed, the capacity of twelve for even divisions.

The importance of this special property of twelve (namely, of being divided equally in many possible ways without splitting unity, or producing a fractional result or remainder) is reflected in its symbolism in the number of apostles, patriarchs, tribes of Israel, etc.

The text of the paragraph above has been paraphrased somewhat in the present translation, for the sake of clarity for contemporary readers.

When the first four numbers which are produced by doubling (that is, one, two, four, and eight) are all added together, the result is sixteen. Moreover, sixteen is the product of multiplying four (which represents solidity or firmness) with itself. For these reasons, certain persons hold that sixteen represents symbolically perfect completeness. Nevertheless, in Sacred Scripture, sixteen appears relatively seldom; and when it does, it does not appear to be assigned such significance. Rather it is the number twelve which occurs very frequently, in the context of this meaning. Thus it is that there are twelve thrones of judgment, and twelve tribes of the people of Israel. These twelve tribes, together with the twelve apostles, represent allegorically or symbolically the peoples of all the nations of earth.

When twelve is multiplied by itself, it produces the number 144. This number is uses to represent the entire Church in the Apocalypse, in which we read of the saved as consisting of a multitude numbering some 144,000 persons—that is, 12,000 from each of the twelve tribes of Israel.[130] We find likewise, as has been noted, twelve patriarchs and twelve apostles. Twelve is likewise the total number of the

[130] See Apocalypse of St. John 7:1–8.

minor prophets. There were twelve varieties of stone which were set in the breastplate of the priests, described in the book of Exodus.[131]

The twelve apostles, through whom flowed forth the teachings of Christ to the world, are foreshadowed mystically in the twelve springs of water at Elim, which the Israelites came upon as they wandered through the desert led by Moses. Watered by these twelve springs, there were growing seventy palm trees[132]—manifesting both the sacred number of seven (signifying the union of the mystery of the divinity and human nature in and through Christ), as well as the law or justice of God, symbolized in the number ten, since seven by ten produce seventy. Thus, from the twelve fonts of apostolic tradition, represented in the passage by the twelve wells, the Gospel of salvation (embodying both the mystery of the Incarnation of the eternal Word, as well as the moral teachings or precepts of Christ, represented by the seventy palm trees) grows forth and is nourished.

Twelve explorers were sent forth by Moses to survey and examine the land of Canaan, which God had pledged to the Israelites as the promised land.[133] And they carried with them a bunch of grapes upon a wooden branch from that land, signifying in this action and object Christ, who is the

[131] See Exodus 28:15–30.
[132] See Exodus 15:26–27.
[133] See Numbers 13.

true vine, and His saving cross. Twelve stones were placed in the River Jordan when the Israelites passed through it and the waters of the river were parted before the Ark of the Covenant.[134] These twelve stones were placed there by Joshua to serve as a perpetual reminded of this marvelous event.

Next, Elijah commanded that the altar of the Lord upon Mount Carmel should also be constructed out of some twelve stones.[135] And when the remaining scraps were collected after Christ had fed the multitude, on one of these occasions, it is recorded that twelve baskets were filled.[136]

Translator's note

It is deeply significant, and by no means coincidental, that after Christ's two miracles of feeding the multitude, on one occasion twelve baskets of leftovers were collected, and on the other occasion, it was seven.[137] *Both twelve and seven are held to be sacred because of each of them mystically symbolizes the union of the mystery of the Godhead (represented by three) with human nature (represented by four)—seven being the result of adding these two numbers together, and twelve being the result of multiplying them with each other. Christ Himself draws attention to the significance of the specific number of baskets which were collected, and asks His apostles to call these to mind.*[138]

---

[134] See Josue 4.
[135] See 1 Kings 8:31.
[136] See Matthew 14:20; Luke 9:17; John 6:13.
[137] See Matthew 15:37; Mark 8:8.
[138] See Matthew 16:9–10; Mark 8:19–21.

In the book of the Apocalypse, we read that 12,000 persons from each of the twelve tribes of Israel were signed on their foreheads.[139] A crown of twelve stars is seen to shine upon the head of the woman who gives birth to the holy Child.[140] And the foundations of the city of the celestial Jerusalem are twelve precious stones, while the city itself is twelve stadia in both length and breadth. This heavenly city possesses some twelve gates in its walls, and these walls are each 144 (i.e., twelve by twelve) cubits in height.[141]

The number twelve, when multiplied by half of itself, six, produces the number seventy-two. Seventy-two was, of course, the number of the disciples sent forth by the Lord to proclaim the Gospel.[142] This number, seventy-two, signifies all the people of the world, for it is traditionally believed that there are a total of seventy-two different languages spoken throughout the earth.

The number twelve is imbued with significance also in the natural order of the created universe. For the course of the year comprises some twelve months. There are twelve winds which circulate the globe of the world; and each day comprises some twelve hours, while each night is likewise divided into the same number of hours.

---

[139] See Revelation 7:4–9.
[140] See Revelation 12:1.
[141] See Revelation 15:21.
[142] See Luke 10:1.

Translator's note

The belief that there was a total of seventy-two languages in the world, corresponding with seventy-two different nations or races, originate with early Christian writers. This number, seventy-two, is linked to, or derived from, the number of grandsons of Noah (according to the Septuagint), who repopulated the world after the flood, each founding a separate nation or race.

Since the time of the classical world (and throughout the Middle Ages), it was believed that there were twelve principal winds in the world—which are listed by Aristotle in his influential treatise on meteorology as Boreas (North), Meses (NNE), Caecias (NE), Apeliotes (E), Eurus (SE), Orthonotus (SSE), Notus (S), Leuconotus (SSW), Lips (SW), Zephyrus (W), Iapyx (NW), and Thracias (NNW).

Traditionally, both the day and the night were divided into twelve hours each, and hence the traditional designations such as "the third hour" or "the sixth hour," etc., to indicate the various times of day. The length of these hours was somewhat variable, according to the duration of the period of sunlight for each day.

EPILOGUE

From a sermon of St. Isidore of Seville in the *Breviarium Romanum ex Decreto SS. Concilii Tridentini Restitutum*

IT IS NECESSARY that whosoever would instruct and lead the people of God in virtue should himself be holy in all respects and not subject to reproach in any way. To such a person, deep knowledge of Sacred Scripture is indispensable. For only if a bishop is learned in both his speech and teaching will he be able to instruct others and to refute error. His discourses ought to be pure, simple, open, and filled with both gravity and grace. It is the special duty of such a person to study the Sacred Scriptures and the canons of the Church; and also to imitate the virtues of the saints, through diligent fasting, prayer, and seeking peace with others.

The one who would lead others ought to offer a prudent balance of humility and authority, neither being excessively submissive or permissive, lest vices are able to flourish, nor being overly severe and harsh. Above all, he ought to hold firmly to the virtue of love, for without this, all the other virtues amount to nothing at all.

A TABLE OF NUMBERS IN THIS BOOK

Arabic	Latin	Greek	Hebrew
1	I	α	א
2	II	β	ב
3	III	γ	ג
4	IV	δ	ד
5	V	ε	ה
6	VI	ς	ו
7	VII	ζ	ז
8	VIII	η	ח
9	IX	θ	ט
10	X	ι	י
11	XI	ια	יא
12	XII	ιβ	יב